VERSAILLES

Photographies : Jacques GIRARD
Jean-Claude VARGA
Bernard DUPONT, René-Paul PAYEN
Plans : Pierre BEQUET, Michel LEFEBVRE
Dominique TOUZOT
Maquette : Jacques GIRARD
Réalisation : Pierre KEGELS
Copyright : Editions d'Art Lys

Photocomposition et Photogravure
BUSSIERE ARTS GRAPHIQUES - Paris
Achevé d'imprimer le 15 Février 1988
B.E. impression
Dépôt légal 2ᵉ trimestre 1985
ISBN 2-85495-007-0

GERALD VAN DER KEMP
Membre de l'Institut
Inspecteur Général Honoraire des Musées

SIMONE HOOG ET DANIEL MEYER
Conservateurs au Musée National
des Châteaux de Versailles et de Trianon

VERSAILLES

THE CHÂTEAU
THE GARDENS
AND TRIANON

Translation: Bronia Fuchs

complete guide

CONTENTS

INTRODUCTION

One must come to Versailles to appreciate the extent of France's influence during the great centuries of its monarchical rule.

As one strolls through this superb setting, one can understand how visitors of long ago marvelled at the architecture, the décors and the wonderful gardens.

The magnificence of Versailles was born of the artistic, spiritual and political power of France and its Kings in the 17th and 18th centuries and, in particular, from 1682 onwards, when Versailles became the permanent Court residence and the country's administrative centre.

The history of the royal estate, which this guidebook invites us to visit, is that of a simple hunting pavilion which was transformed first into a country residence and then enlarged to become a veritable château surrounded by gardens.

It was later completed by the creation of a town and finally chosen as the permanent home of the sovereign and his court and as the seat of government.

The four Kings who reigned over France from 1610 to 1789 made more or less far-reaching changes to the château and its outhouses,

Louis XIV
by Rigaud

each according to his taste and concept of a château.

Relatively little is known of the original hunting pavilion which Louis XIII (1601-1643) had erected in 1623 on the hill overlooking the village of Versailles to the north: "a miserable construction of which a simple gentleman would not boast", says Bassompierre.

However, it was so pleasantly situated that, in 1631, Louis XIII asked Philibert Le Roy to build a larger château, entirely of brick and stone, with raised slate roofing, the remains of which may be admired in the Marble Courtyard.

When the King died in 1643, his wife, Anne of Austria, was forced by the political vicissitudes of the *Fronde* to change her place of residence continually and move, with the young Louis XIV (1638-1715), between Paris and Saint-Germain-en-Laye.

Louis XIV, enchanted by the little château of Versailles, decided as early as 1661 to devote every possible care to having it renovated so that he could live there more comfortably.

Le Nôtre (1613-1700), the gardener, Le Vau (1612-1670), the head architect and Le Brun (1619-1690), the head painter, spent all their time on enlarging and embellishing Versailles.

The visual arts were no longer sufficient to decorate this estate. Louis XIV also wished to add the prestige offered by Music and Literature. With this aim in mind, the King held three unforgettable festivities in ten years.

The first of these, "The Pleasures of the Enchanted Island", took place in May 1664; the King secretly dedicated it to Mademoiselle de La Vallière.

The theme of the celebrations was taken from two older works of literature, "Orlando Furioso" by Ariosto and "Gerusalemme liberata" by Tasso. Molière produced "The Princess of Elis" and the first three acts of "Tartuffe". The second celebration, and the most famous of the trilogy, was held on 18th July 1668; it is known as the "Great Royal Entertainment of Versailles" and was marked by the creation of two works, "Georges Dandin" by Molière and "Les Fêtes de l'Amour et de Bacchus" by Lully. The last great celebration was held by Louis XIV at Versailles in July 1674. It included several operas by Lully (Alceste, the Eclogue of Versailles, Les Fêtes de l'Amour et de Bacchus), Molière produced "Le Malade Imaginaire" and, on 18th August, Racine's "Iphigenia" was performed in the Orangery.

When the buildings in the entrance courtyard had been erected and the parterres were beginning to take form, Colbert protested and tried to convince Louis XIV to pay more attention to the Louvre, the traditional palace of the Kings of France since Philippe August, but his pleas remained unsuccessful.

In 1668, after the Great Royal Entertainment, Louis XIV decided to enlarge Versailles "in order to live there comfortably with his Council for several days... The three large buildings around the small château were constructed, looking on to the gardens; they were designed by M. Le Vau" (Ch. Perrault).

Louis XIII's château is therefore surrounded on three sides (1664-1670) by Le Vau's buildings. In the newly built northern section the King's State Apartments were created, on the southern side, those of the Queen, with a large terrace between them, overlooking the gardens.

On the courtyard side, the ditches were filled in and the wings connected to the kitchens and stables by new buildings of brick and stone.

The new courtyard, which was more than twice the size of the Marble Courtyard of Louis XIII's residence, was closed off by a semicircular railing. Beyond, in the corners of the large entrance courtyard, stood four pavilions which Mansart linked to create the Ministers' Wings.

Shortly after Le Vau's death (1670), Jules Hardouin-Mansart (1646-1708), great-nephew of the great architect of the first half of the 17th century, François Mansart, took over the direction of construction.

His desire for architectural grandeur corresponded completely to the Sun King's taste in buildings. After Le Brun's death in 1690, he became the all-powerful master of the King's buildings at Versailles.

He extended the façade on the park side: the terrace was replaced by the large ensemble formed by the War Drawing Room, the Peace Drawing Room and the Hall of Mirrors.

To the north and south, Mansart had two wings containing apartments erected between 1682 and 1686. On the Marble Courtyard side, another storey was added to the small château. It contained three windows three windows and a clock. On the garden side the château façade was now roughly 2200 feet long.

Inside the château, Mansart built the Queen's Staircase in the south section to match the Ambassadors' Staircase begun by Le Vau in the north wing and which was to be destroyed in 1752.

The King's apartments overlooking the Marble Courtyard were then altered and given their present form with the King's Bedchamber in the centre of the château, with by the Bull's Eye Drawing-Room and the Council Cabinet on either side.

In 1699, Mansart began construction of the Royal Chapel, inaugurated by the King in 1710, two years after the death of the great architect, whose work was taken over and completed by his brother-in-law, Robert de Cotte (1656-1735).

Upon Louis XIV's death in 1715, the Versailles of our day had already taken shape in its general outward appearance. The successors of the great King altered only the interior décor of the apartments.

In 1722, Louis XV (1710-1774), Louis XIV's great-grandson, made Versailles the royal residence once more; new construction work was undertaken in 1733 and the Hercules Drawing Room, inaugurated in 1736, received its splendid ceiling, painted by Lemoine.

The King's private apartments on the first floor of the northern secton overlooking the Marble Courtyard were decorated in a more intimate style. For this reason, Louis XIV's Cabinet of Curios and Rare Objects was destroyed, and, later, the Ambassadors' Staircase.

Although the changes made by Louis XV involved the disappearance of some of the rooms which were such a source of wonder to visitors of Louis XIV's time, they resulted, nevertheless, in the creation of the King's charming cabinets

In these rooms, the artists surpassed themselves in their zeal and elegance as they worked under the direction of the architect and decorator Jacques-Ange Gabriel, in whom the King had placed his confidence.

It was the same architect who, after several projects had remained incomplete, built the fine Opera of Versailles in twenty-one months, in the north wing of the château. It was inaugurated in 1770 for the marriage of the Dauphin to the Archduchess Marie-Antoinette.

Gabriel then decided to reconstruct the courtyard side of the château. All that remains of his project is the wing which is named after him, with a classical frenton supported by a colonnade to the right of the entrance courtyard. Under the Restoration, Dufour had a matching pavilion erected; today, it houses the curator's offices.

Unlike his ancestors, Louis XVI (1754-1793) took no great interest

Louis XV
by Rigaud

in further construction work and the only changes made were to the palace interior. The most noteworthy of these concerned the Queen's private suite which was developed at the same time as the Queen's State Apartment on the south side of the Marble Courtyard. Marie-Antoinette had a series of small cabinets created there, following the example of Maria Leczinska.

After the revolution of July 1830, which brought Louis-Philippe d'Orléans (1773-1850) to power, the Chamber of Deputies voted a law placing the estate of Versailles and Trianon on the Civil List. Almost immediately, Louis-Philippe ordered the creation at Versailles of a Museum dedicated "To all the Glories of France" wich was inaugurated on 1st June 1837. Today Versailles continues to play its part as a historical museum. In the North Wing, the 17th century rooms form an introduction to the tour of the State Apartments which may be continued by visiting the Hall of Battles and the rooms in the south wing dedicated to the Napoleonic Epoque. With the renovation of the 18th and 19th century rooms, this vast panorama of our history will be complete.

Each of the sovereigns who lived at Versailles left his mark. The vast estate of the palace, park and

Trianon hold countless treasures both for the curious visitor and the art historian.

The transition is easily made from Louis XIII's château with its poetic brick and stone façade, so close in inspiration to the art of the late 16th century, to 17th century classical art, to which we owe this spacious palace with its Italian style terraces. The rich décor of Louis XIV's period was refined and given grace and charm by the alterations made by Louis XV and Louis XVI, a triumph of the 18th century spirit in all its variety. The observant visitor may thus follow the extremely rich development of French art. Despite the traces left by its inhabitants and their widely diverging tastes, the palace gives an overall impression of the greatest unity and harmony.

It was in this glorious setting that the sovereigns of Versailles lived. The King's life was regulated to the minutest detail by the laws of Etiquette. The King's every action and gesture were the pretext for a ceremony: his rising and retiring, his meal or his walk in the gardens. A dazzling audience was present when the King heard mass or granted an audience to an ambassador and the Court filled the palace with a life and vitality now lost forever.

To entertain their courtiers, the

Louis XVI
by Callet

Kings held magnificent festivities which, in the words of Louis XIV, ''were not so much their own as those of a whole people''. They consisted of theatrical performances, operas and masked or full-dress balls held in the apartments, the Hall of Mirrors or the park; in Marie-Antoinette's time, Trianon was the theatre for many *illuminations* in which the park was embellished with special lighting. These festivities were the wonder of Europe, where every King wished to live the French style. The economic importance of Versailles became obvious and it was made a permanent centre for the exhibition of articles produced in French manufactury. In Russia, Peter the Great created a new city in the style of Versailles: Saint Petersburg. Later, Catherine the Great had hundreds of works of art bought in Paris: paintings, sculptures, tapestries, furniture, porcelain and silverware. Architects throughout Europe found their source of inspiration at Versailles for the new palaces their sovereigns had ordered them to build; some of the many court residences created in this way were Sans-Souci, Potsdam, Schoenbrunn and Caserta. During the last century, Louis II of Bavaria had the central building of the château and the parterres in the gardens reproduced at Herrenchiemsee. The visitor walking through the drawing rooms of Versailles never feels overcome by the profusion of gold, marble, bronze and mirrors, for, throughout the palace, the sense of luxury has been heightened with artistry. In the gardens, the parterres with their embroidery of colourful flowers, the paths lined with marble statues and carved fountains, everything echoes the splendour of the palace though on a larger scale: it extends into infinity, beyond the view of the Royal Avenue and the sparkling waters of the Grand Canal. After the departure of the monarchy, the art of Versailles came to an almost entire halt. However, by means of important technical achievements, an attempt is being made in our time to revive the royal estate as completely as possible.

Of course, many changes made during the 19th century altered the château interior but, today, the Curatorial and Architecture Departments of Versailles are attempting to restore life to it by gradually refurnishing the rooms which the Revolution had emptied of their furniture and by patiently restoring and consolidating the structure of this monument which time and past indifference did not spare.

The château around 1722 painted by Pierre-Denis Martin

THE CHATEAU

A DESCRIPTION OF THE PALACE
ON THE TOWN SIDE

The visitor who comes to Versailles cannot lose his way: three huge avenues lead him to the Palace: the Avenue de Paris (opposite the château), the Avenue de Saint-Cloud (to the North) and the Avenue de Sceaux (to the south). On reaching the Royal Parade Ground, the Avenue de Paris is flanked by the Great Stables (to the north), and the Small Stables (to the south) erected by Mansart. Along these avenues, which are planted with trees, run lanes lined with 17th and 18th century mansions and buildings. Leaving the Royal Parade Ground behind him, the visitor comes to the main entrance, with its railings bearing the Royal Arms of France and adorned with Apollo's lyres. The Great Courtyard is flanked by the two Ministers' Wings (built by Le Vau and Mansart) and closed off by the entrance gate to the east; to the west, there used to be another set of railings which were destroyed during the Revolution, on the site of the present Equestrian Statue of Louis XIV, dating from 1837.

The Royal Courtyard was separated from the Marble Courtyard by a flight of five steps. Only a restricted number of coaches were allowed to go further, those belonging to the lords who had the right to the "Honours of the Louvre".

The entrance gate, no longer in existence, was linked to two pavilions, later destroyed, which were replaced by the Louis XV Wing, to the right, and by the

Dufour Pavilion (erected under Louis XVIII), to the left. Behind the Dufour Pavilion, in the same alignment, there stands the Old Wing, dating from 1662. Further on, to the left, the visitor now discovers a series of three gilded railings opening out into the lobby of the Queen's Staircase; the railings to the right once gave access to the lobby of the Ambassadors' Staircase, (which was pulled down in 1752).

The Marble Courtyard becomes more and more narrow owing to the projecting façades of the buildings.

At the end of the courtyard eight columns of Rance Marble support the balcony of Louis XIV's Chamber. The constructions surrounding the Marble Courtyard once made up Louis XIII's Château.

Over the last few years attempts have been made to restore these courtyards to their former appearance.

The Marble Courtyard was recently raised to its original level and given a pavement relatively close to its former 17th century one.

One hopes that, in time to come, the equestrian statue of Louis XIV will be removed and the railings which once separated the Great Courtyard and the Royal Courtyard returned here.

The Palace
seen from the air

On arriving at this spot, the visitor should stop a moment to dream of the time when these buildings still existed in all their colour, when the stone was golden, the brick red, and the lead ornamentation of the roofing covered in gold leaf.

*The Courtyard in front of the château around 1690
by Jean-Baptiste Martin*

13

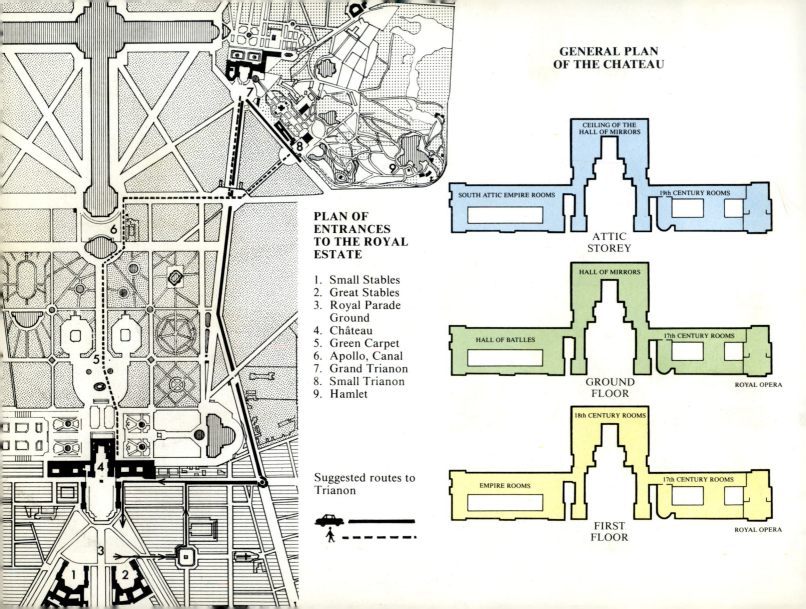

PLAN OF ENTRANCES TO THE ROYAL ESTATE

1. Small Stables
2. Great Stables
3. Royal Parade Ground
4. Château
5. Green Carpet
6. Apollo, Canal
7. Grand Trianon
8. Small Trianon
9. Hamlet

Suggested routes to Trianon

GENERAL PLAN OF THE CHATEAU

CEILING OF THE HALL OF MIRRORS

SOUTH ATTIC EMPIRE ROOMS

19th CENTURY ROOMS

ATTIC STOREY

HALL OF MIRRORS

HALL OF BATLLES

17th CENTURY ROOMS

GROUND FLOOR

ROYAL OPERA

18th CENTURY ROOMS

EMPIRE ROOMS

17th CENTURY ROOMS

FIRST FLOOR

ROYAL OPERA

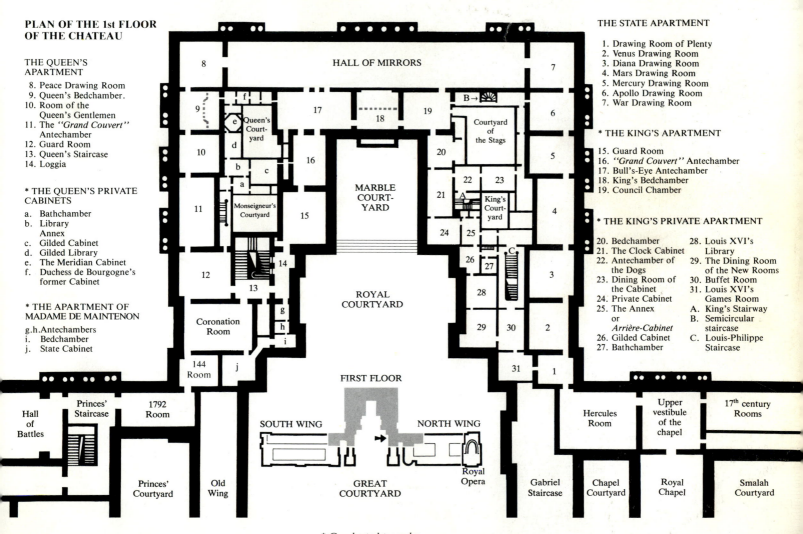

PLAN OF THE 1st FLOOR OF THE CHATEAU

THE QUEEN'S APARTMENT

8. Peace Drawing Room
9. Queen's Bedchamber.
10. Room of the Queen's Gentlemen
11. The *"Grand Couvert"* Antechamber
12. Guard Room
13. Queen's Staircase
14. Loggia

* THE QUEEN'S PRIVATE CABINETS

a. Bathchamber
b. Library Annex
c. Gilded Cabinet
d. Gilded Library
e. The Meridian Cabinet
f. Duchess de Bourgogne's former Cabinet

* THE APARTMENT OF MADAME DE MAINTENON

g.h. Antechambers
i. Bedchamber
j. State Cabinet

THE STATE APARTMENT

1. Drawing Room of Plenty
2. Venus Drawing Room
3. Diana Drawing Room
4. Mars Drawing Room
5. Mercury Drawing Room
6. Apollo Drawing Room
7. War Drawing Room

* THE KING'S APARTMENT

15. Guard Room
16. *"Grand Couvert"* Antechamber
17. Bull's-Eye Antechamber
18. King's Bedchamber
19. Council Chamber

* THE KING'S PRIVATE APARTMENT

20. Bedchamber
21. The Clock Cabinet
22. Antechamber of the Dogs
23. Dining Room of the Cabinet
24. Private Cabinet
25. The Annex or *Arrière-Cabinet*
26. Gilded Cabinet
27. Bathchamber
28. Louis XVI's Library
29. The Dining Room of the New Rooms
30. Buffet Room
31. Louis XVI's Games Room
A. King's Stairway
B. Semicircular staircase
C. Louis-Philippe Staircase

HALL OF MIRRORS

8 7 9 17 18 19 6 5 Courtyard of the Stags 20 22 23 4 21 King's Courtyard 24 25 26 27 28 29 30 3 31 2 1

Queen's Courtyard

Monseigneur's Courtyard

MARBLE COURT-YARD

ROYAL COURTYARD

Coronation Room

144 Room j g h i 15 10 11 12 13 14 16 A B→ C

FIRST FLOOR

SOUTH WING → **NORTH WING**

Royal Opera

Hall of Battles

Princes' Staircase

1792 Room

Princes' Courtyard

Old Wing

GREAT COURTYARD

Hercules Room

Upper vestibule of the chapel

17th century Rooms

Gabriel Staircase

Chapel Courtyard

Royal Chapel

Smalah Courtyard

* Conducted tours by National Museum guides

15

THE 17th CENTURY ROOMS

After crossing the entrance hall, called the Gabriel Vestibule, and the Lower Chapel Vestibule, the tour of the château begins with the rooms on the ground floor and the first floor of the north wing on the garden side. The rooms in this part of the château were at one time apartments for the princes, but were destroyed when Louis-Philippe transformed Versailles into a museum.

After a first room featuring 16th century portraits from the Gaignières Collection, these rooms contain 17th century iconography and therefore make up an appropriate introduction to the history of the château.

After the reigns of Louis XIV's predecessors, the visitor will see depictions of the regency of Anne of Austria, *the Fronde* and the Jansenist movement, the first artists of Versailles and France's foreign policy at the beginning of Louis XIV's reign.

The young King wished to add to his military and diplomatic successes the prestige of a refined civilization, and had the good fortune of seeing a host of talented artists gather to work at his court. The various stages in the construction of Versailles are illustrated in paintings like that of Patel.

"Entry into Arras" (detail)
by Adam Van der Meulen

The last rooms conjure up Court life, its receptions, its festivities, the brilliant entourage of the young ruler and, finally, interest in the development of the sciences.

Two rooms on the first floor contain works depicting different episodes from Louis XIV's wars.

The Court followed the army as it moved around.

The views of the Royal Châteaux are a reminder of the King's passion for building. These are followed by portraits of painters and sculptors who worked on their decoration. Louis XIV's intimate entourage, his ministers and the royal family are portrayed in the following rooms where several masterpieces by Mignard are displayed.

In the last room before the upper Chapel Vestibule, a large tapestry cartoon of the audience granted by Louis XIV to the Doge of Genoa at Versailles on 15th May 1685 depicts the King in the Hall of Mirrors, still adorned with the silver furniture which was to be melted down in 1689.

Not all the works exhibited here are of equal quality. However, an attempt has been made, here as in the rest of the museum, to present only sculptures and paintings contemporaneous with the events illustrated.

The château around 1668
painted by Pierre Patel

THE CHAPEL

The Royal Chapel of Versailles is situated near the angle formed by the château's central section and the north wing, on the city side. This is the château's fifth chapel, but the first to occupy a separate building, as the earlier ones had always formed part of the château itself.

It was constructed by Jules Hardouin-Mansart from 1699 until his death in 1708 and completed in 1710 by his brother-in-law, Robert de Cotte. It has two storeys, like the traditional Palatine chapels, but its style is classical in inspiration.

The vestibule leading to it on the ground floor is adorned with Ionic order columns. The fine white stone comes from the quarries of Créteil. On the chapel floor, marble of various colours forms a magnificent carpet with large geometrical compartments; in the middle of the nave are the royal arms and in front of the altar steps the King's monogram: two L's intertwined beneath a crown. The ground floor is surrounded by arcades of massive square pillars; a Corinthian colonnade runs around the upper storey.

The Chapel was dedicated to Saint-Louis. According to tradi-

The Royal Chapel
the main altar

tion, the decorative theme brings out the parallel between the Old and New Testaments.

The Coustou brothers, Frémin, Lemoine, Van Clève, Magnier, Poirier, Vassé, etc., adorned the chapel with religious objects on either side of the ground floor pillars, angels bearing the attributes of the Passion in the corners of the arcades, bas-reliefs on the high altar of marble and gilt-bronze, on the organ loft by Robert Cliquot, overdoors in the royal gallery, etc.

The ceiling paintings represent the Holy Trinity. In the centre, above the nave, ''The Eternal Father announcing to the world the coming of the Messiah'', by Antoine Coypel, is surrounded by paintings of architectural forms by Philippe Meusnier. ''The Resurrection of Christ'', over the altar, in the rounded vault, is the work of Charles de Lafosse.

Finally, the royal gallery opposite the altar is surmounted by ''The Holy Spirit descending on the Apostles'', by Jouvenet. The original Savonnerie carpet, with the arms of France in its centre, was returned here in 1957.

The King of France would hear mass from the gallery which was on the same floor as his apartments. He entered the lower half of the chapel only when a bishop officiated.

This chapel was the setting for the ceremonies of the Order of the Holy Spirit, the Te Deum was sung here for military victories and births of the Children of France, and the Princes of the Blood were married here. The most important of these marriages were that of the Duc de Berry in 1710, of the Dauphin, Louis XV's son, who married first the Infanta, Maria-Teresa of Spain, in 1745 and then Maria-Josepha of Saxony in 1747, that of the future Dauphin, Louis XVI, to Marie-Antoinette in 1770 and of the future Kings, Louis XVIII in 1771 and Charles V in 1774.

The Chapel
ceiling

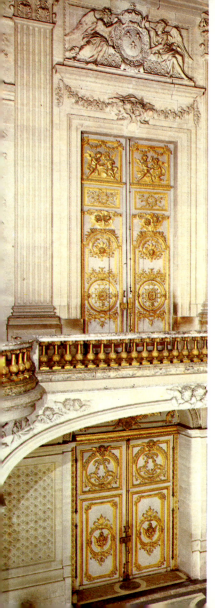

The Royal
Gallery

THE UPPER CHAPEL VESTIBULE

The Vestibule was built at the same time as the Chapel; it continues its stone décor and connects it to the State Apartment.
The only ornamental elements in this vestibule are the sculptured motifs.

Columns and pilasters with Corinthian capitals support the vaulted ceiling adorned with stucco medallions in the corners portraying the four parts of the world. Above the doors and windows are arches with carved figures of Virtues by Poirier, La Pierre, G. Coustou and Poulletier. One of the two niches contains the statue of Glory holding a medallion of Louis XV, by Vassé, the other the statue of Magnanimity, by Bousseau.

THE HERCULES DRAWING ROOM

This huge room, the château's largest, is a passageway linking the north wing and the central building.

It was created in the upper section of the fourth chapel (used from 1682 to 1710). The decoration was entrusted to Robert de Cotte, who began the task in 1712. It was interrupted in 1715 by the death of Louis XIV and only resumed in 1725. The walls are covered with marble of different hues and rythmed with twenty pilasters with gilt-bronze pedestals and Corinthian capitals. They support a cornice adorned with consoles and trophies. The fireplace of Antin marble is decorated with chased gilt bronzes by Antoine Vassé. Above it hangs Veronese's "Eliezer and Rebecca". Another painting by Veronese hangs opposite it: "The Meal in the House of Simon the Pharisee"; it was presented to Louis XIV by the Venetian Republic in 1664.

The décor was designed to match these two works by Veronese, particularly the ceiling, painted by François Lemoine from 1733 to 1736. It portays the Apotheosis of Hercules and was so greatly admired that the artist was named

Ceiling by François Lemoine in the Hercules Drawing-Room

"Christ's meal at the house of Simon"
by Veronese

Head Painter to the King. This room was the setting for receptions on great occasions such as the full dress ball of 1739.

"Lemoine's work consists of nine groups comprising 142 figures (...). In the first, Jupiter and Juno present Hercules, her future husband, to the young Hebe. Bacchus may be seen leaning on the god Pan in the second group. Above them are Amphitrite and Mercury, and, lower down, Venus with the Graces and Eros, Pandora and Diana... The third group consists of Mars, Vulcan and cupids (...) Envy, Anger, Hatred, Discord and other Vices, brought to the ground beside Hercules' chariot, make up the fourth group. The fifth shows Cybele in a chariot, Minerva and Ceres, Neptune and Pluto. In the sixth, one can see Aeolus, Zephyr and Flora, Dew inclining over her urn on the clouds (...), below, Dreams spread poppies over the sleeping Morpheus (...). The seventh group represents Iris with Dawn surrounded by four Stars personified. Apollo with his Muses compose the eigth group (...) while, in the ninth, the constellations of Castor and Pollux and Silenus followed by a band of children and fauns hold a Bacchanalean revelry in honour of Hercules."

(Dezallier d'Argenville)

The Hercules Drawing-Room
detail of the ceiling

THE STATE APARTMENT

The State Apartment, on the first floor of the château, overlooks the North Parterre. It was begun in 1671 and completed in 1681. It comprises seven rooms whose purpose was not defined until 1682 when the King made Versailles his Court and seat of government. This apartment, "where the King receives but does not live", was entered from the Ambassadors' Staircase whose two flights led to the Venus and Diana Drawing Rooms. The Ambassadors' Staircase, decorated, like the State Apartment, by Le Brun, was destroyed in 1752 for the creation of the King's private apartment overlooking the Marble Courtyard. The King's State Apartment unfolds in a lavish suite of rooms dedicated to mythological themes, described by Félibien in 1674: "Since the Sun is the King's emblem, the seven planets were taken as the subjects of the paintings in the seven rooms which compose this apartment".

THE DRAWING ROOM OF PLENTY

When the Chapel occupied the site of the Hercules Drawing

The Drawing Room of Plenty

"The King allows his State Apartment to be entered... on Mondays, Wednesdays and Thursdays of each week... from six o'clock in the evening until ten, and these days are called Appartement days. One may speak with complete freedom... The King, Queen and all the Royal House step down from their positions of grandeur to play with several of the guests, who have never been honoured in this manner".

Room, this room served as an entrance hall to the galleries. It also gave access to the Cabinet of Curios and Rare Objects. The collections it contained inspired the décor of the ceiling, the work of René-Antoine Houasse, a pupil of Le Brun; in the centre is an allegory of Royal Magnificence, surrounded by pieces of the gold plate set out on a simulated balustrade.

Over the door is an oval medallion containing an image of Magnificence in gold monochrome.

This room, like the following one, was decorated with doorhangings and stools of green velvet galloned with gold. For this reason in 1955, the walls were once again covered with the gold-fringed Genoan velvet, rewoven after 17th century models.

In 1975, the patinated bronze busts of characters from Antiquity were returned here. The sumptuous Boulle marquetry cabinets are a reminder of the furniture of Louis XIV's time.

Visitors may admire the portraits of the Sun King's descendants: the Duc d'Anjou, who became Philip V of Spain, the Grand Dauphin, his father, and his brother, the Duc de Bourgogne, all three painted by Rigaud, and the Duc de Bourgogne's son, Louis XV, by J.-B. Van Loo.

"Royal Magnificence"
ceiling painted by R.-A. Houasse

THE VENUS DRAWING ROOM

This and the following room were reached by the Ambassadors' Staircase, demolished in 1752.

The name of the Venus Drawing Room comes from the ceiling painting, the work of R.-A. Houasse, representing "Venus Subjugating the Gods and Powers". The oval in the centre portrays Venus in her chariot, crowned by the three Graces. She holds garlands of roses entwined around Mars, Vulcan, Bacchus, Neptune and Jupiter. These garlands extend into the corners of the ceiling, where they are used by cupids to ensnare Titus and Berenice, Antony and Cleopatra, Jason and Medea and Theseus and Ariadne. On either side of the central motif, two monochrome paintings on a gold background depict "The Abduction of Europa by Jupiter metamorphosed into a Bull", and "Amphitrite on a Dolphin's Back".

The classical themes on the coves evoke great events of Louis XIV's reign: "Augustus presiding over the Circus Games", recalls the 1662 *Carroussel* celebrations; "Nebuchadnezzar and Semiramis and the creation of the Hanging Gardens of Babylon", finds its counterpart in the work undertaken for the Royal Estates; "Alexander's Marriage to Roxana" calls to mind the King's marriage; "Cyrus taking arms to rescue a Princess" is a reminder of the war for the Queen's hereditary claims in 1667.

Against the far wall and framing the doors are marble columns and pilasters of the Ionic order.

The painted perspectives on the side walls are by Jacques Rousseau who also painted the *trompe-l'œil* statues of Meleager and Atalanta between the windows.

A niche in the middle of the far wall opposite the windows contains the statue of the young Louis XIV, by Jean Warin. The King is represented

"The supremacy of Venus"
ceiling by R.-A. Houasse

in full length, clothed in classical military costume; in his right hand he holds the *bâton de commandement* leaning against a cuirass and his left hand rests on a helmet in the shape of a lion's mouth, placed on a shield ornamented with a Gorgon's head. Eight classical busts have been placed here until the original ones are found. It was here that, on *Appartement* evenings, the light supper was served on tables set out along the walls. The room was lit by two large silver chande-- liers and eight crystal candelabra on gilded pedestal tables. The fabric used for the doors and stools was a green velvet gallooned with gold.

The Venus Drawing-Room

THE DIANA DRAWING ROOM

Louis XIV first used this room as a Billiards Room. In the centre stood the billiards table, covered with gold-fringed velvet, and platforms covered with Persian carpets embroidered in gold and silver were placed around the room for the ladies to sit and watch the game.

Through Félibien, we know that Louis XIV, who was an impressive billardsplayer, had this room furnished with *"four large silver chandeliers and four candlesticks also of silver... in the corners of a billiard table"*.

The ceiling painting portrays "Diana (Apollo's sister) in her chariot watching over hunting and navigation.

The goddess is surrounded by allegories of the nocturnal hours (one reading a book and the other sent to sleep by Cupid showering her with poppies) and the early morning hours spreading flowers and dew round about. This painting is the work of Gabriel Blanchard who also executed the monochrome overdoors, each of which evokes an episode from the legend and cult of the goddess of the hunt: "Diana and Actaeon", "Diana protecting Arethusa", "A Floral Offering" and "A Sacrifice to Diana".

Ceiling
of the Diana Drawing Room

Two different artists painted the coves. "Jason and the Argonauts", over the fireplace, and "Alexander hunting lions", above the windows, are by Charles de Lafosse, while "Cyrus hunting wild boar" and "Julius Caesar sending a Roman settlement to Carthage" are the work of Claude Audran.

In 1685, Louis XIV had his bust by Bernini, carved twenty years earlier, placed in this room. He had gilt-bronze ornamentation added to the walls: trophies and winged children bearing the royal crown. The models for these reliefs were created by Mazeline and Jouvenet and they were cast by the Keller brothers.

Above the fireplace hangs a painting by Charles de Lafosse representing The "Iphigenia being rescued by Diana just as she is about to be sacrificed". A small marble bas-relief attributed to Jacques Sarrazin is set into the chimney-piece. Its subject is "The Flight into Egypt". In a painting adorning the opposite wall, Gabriel Blanchard has portrayed the goddess who, "forgetting her resolution never to fall in love, goes to Endymion". In 1975, eight classical busts with heads of marble or porphyry, some of which belonged to the former décor, were placed on marble stands along the walls.

Diana Drawing Room: Louis XIV bust by Gian Lorenzo Bernini

THE MARS DRAWING ROOM

The military décor of this room is explained by the fact that it first served as a guard room. It was here that the Bodyguards responsible for protecting the monarch were stationed.

In the centre of the ceiling, "Mars in a wolf-drawn chariot", by Audran, is flanked by "Hercules supporting Victory", by Jouvenet, and "Terror, Fear and Horror overwhelming the Earthly Powers", by Houasse. In the coves, monochrome medallions by Audran, Jouvenet and Houasse depict the exploits of Caesar, Cyrus, Demetrius, Constantine, Alexander Severus and Antony.

Under Louis XIV, this room was embellished with a sumptuous suite of silver furniture, which was melted down in 1689 to meet the cost of the war of the Augsburg League.

It was here that the games took place on *Appartement* evenings.

A concert or ball would follow, for which the musicians sat in two marble galleries with Ionic columns on either side of the fireplace.

On the walls hang a number of very famous paintings : "The Pilgrims of Emmaus" by Veronese, "The Family of

Darius at the feet of Alexander" by Le Brun. The well-known painting of "David playing the Harp" by Domenichino which, at the time of Louis XIV decorated his Chamber alcove, has been hung over the fireplace. In the 18th century, one could admire, on the side walls, two magnificent State portraits of Louis XV (by L.M. Van Loo) and Maria Leczinska (by C. Van Loo). The latter portrait, in which the Queen is clothed in sumptuous court dress, was returned here in 1975. That of the King has unfortunately disappeared. It was replaced by another portrait of the King, also by Van Loo. The floor is covered with a carpet woven under Louis XV by the Savonnerie Manufactory for the Louvre Gallery.

Ceiling
of the Mars Drawing Room

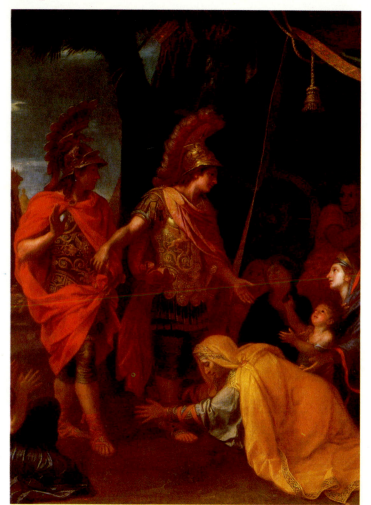

The two porphyry vases were already in the Mars Drawing Room under Louis XIV From 1743 until the Revolution the walls were hung with crimson damask during the summer both in this room and the next two rooms The overdoors symbolize Temperance, Justice, Strength, and Prudence. These four paintings by Simon Vouet are from the Saint-Germain-en-Laye château.

Detail from the painting by Charles Le Brun "The Family of Darius at the feet of Alexander"

THE MERCURY DRAWING ROOM

The entire ceiling of this drawing-room was painted by Jean-Baptiste de Champaigne (1631-1681). The central painting depicts ''Mercury in a chariot drawn by two cocks, preceded by the Morning Star and accompanied by the Arts and Sciences''.

The paintings on the coves are of ''Alexander receiving Indian Ambassadors'', ''Ptolemy in conversation with scientists'' and ''Alexander having foreign animals brought to Aristotle for his study of natural history''. This room was first used as an antechamber and then as the state bedchamber. The bed, covered with richly embroidered fabrics and surmounted by a domed canopy, stood at the end of the room, behind a silver balustrade. The rest of the furniture was also of silver, but it was all melted down in 1689.

On the walls, covered with sumptuous brocades, hung famous paintings, in particular by Titian, which are today in the Louvre. Only one piece of furniture was able to be returned here: the well-known clock presented to Louis XIV by Antoine Morand in 1706.

The upper part of the case, of marquetry adorned with gilt chased bronze, is enclosed in glass on all sides. One can therefore see the mechanism and, in front, a small full-length statue of the King, crowned by a Victory, around which automatons move at set times: beneath the human-faced Rhodian Sun, the King's emblem, clouds part, doors open to reveal laughing dwarfs holding bells which are struck by cupids armed with clubs, etc. Below, the gilt-bronze dial with enamel figures is adorned with an allegory of Time, an old, winged man sitting with a scythe in his hand.

The ceiling
of the Mercury Drawing Room

It was in this room that, on Appartement evenings, the King's games were held.

The Duc d'Anjou, Louis XIV's grandson, was declared King of Spain on 16th November 1700 under the name of Philip V.

To honor the new King, Louis XIV gave him his State Apartment to live in until he left for his new kingdom. This is how Philip V came to occupy this room until 4th December.

Louis XIV slept here in July 1701 while his new bedchamber overlooking the Marble Courtyard was being completed. After his death, his coffin was displayed here from 2nd to 10th September, 1715. Each day, from 5:00 am until midday, seventy-two priests in turn said mass on four altars, one placed in front of the fireplace, another opposite and two more in the window recesses.

The paintings above the doors are of "Apollo and Daphné" by A. Coypel and "Acis and Galatea" by Corneille. On the walls are portraits of the Princes of the family of Louis XV, his three oldest daughters, Mesdames Henriette, Elisabeth and Adelaïde, by Nattier, his son the Dauphin Louis, by Natoire and the latter's first wife, Marie-Thérèse Raphaelle of Spain by Tocqué.

The Mercury Drawing Room

In this Drawing Room, like the one which follows, paintings of great quality hanging on the walls covered in silks with a gold and silver background played their part in creating a dazzling luxury which has since vanished. They were all masterpieces and are today in the Louvre. In the Mercury Drawing-Room the "Holy Family" and "Saint Michael" by Raphael hung beside the "Disciples of Emmaeus" and the "Deposition" by Titian, Caravaggio's "Gipsy Girl", Spada's "Concert" etc…

THE APOLLO DRAWING ROOM

This extraordinarily sump-tuous drawing-room which was the climax to the State Apartment was also where the throne stood.

The ceiling is the work of Charles de Lafosse, a pupil of Le Brun.

The central motif, supported by eight carved and gilded aerial figures shows "Apollo in his chariot in the company of the seasons".

Between the Four Parts of the World in the corners of the archings, the royal grandeur is glorified by classical themes: "Coriolanus lifting the seige of Rome at the request of Veturia, his mother", "Vespasien ordering the construction of the Coliseum", "Augustus having the port of Mysene created" and "Porus brought before Alexander".

The lower section of the walls is covered by panels of marble from Carrara which was called Egyptian marble. The fabrics above varied according to the season. In winter, they were of crimson velvet with eighteen strips of gold and silver em-broidery portraying terms bearing baskets on their heads; between the terms hung "La Tomirice", by Rubens, a "Saint Francis", by Valentin, four "Labours of Hercules", by Guido Reni, "The Virgin and the Donors" and "The Palatine Princes", by Van Dyck. In summer, the walls were covered with gold and silver embroidery. The throne was placed at the end of the room on a dais covered with a Persian carpet with a gold background beneath a canopy of which the three bolts may still be seen.

It was in this Throne Room that the King granted audiences to ambassadors. On *Apparte-ment* evenings, however, music and dance filled the room.

Over the doors, the paintings by Van Dyck have been replaced by "An Allegory of the Dauphin's birth", painted in 1664 by Gabriel Blanchard and a "Figure of Fame spreading the King's glory to the four corners of the earth".

The ceiling of the Apollo Drawing Room

Since
the 18th century
the portrait
of Louis XIV
by Rigaud
hung across
from the
portrait of
the reigning King.
This is why,
across from the
portrait of
the Great King over
the chimney, was
hung the portrait
of Louis XVI
by Callet,
Louis XVI being
the last King
to reside
at Versailles.
The candelabra
had been ordered
by Louis XV
in 1769 for the
Hall of Mirrors.
The floor
is covered with
a 17th century
Savonnerie carpet
adorned
with two
Rhodian suns, the
King's monogram
and motto,
allegories, arms
and magnificent
foliated scrollwork
in the corners.

*The Apollo
Drawing Room*

THE WAR DRAWING ROOM

Jules Hardouin-Mansart began work on the War Drawing-Room in 1678. Its décor, completed by Le Brun in 1686, celebrates the military victories which led to the Peace of Nimeguen.

The walls are lined with marble panels adorned with six gilt-bronze trophies and a cascade of weapons.

On the wall on the Apollo Drawing Room side is a huge stucco bas-relief of "Louis XIV on horseback crushing his enemies underfoot and crowned by Glory". This masterpiece by Coysevox is surmounted by two figures of Fame and held up by two captives bound with chains of flowers. Below, on a bas-relief set into a false fireplace, Clio writes the King's History for posterity.

The ceiling was painted by Le Brun. In the centre, "France, armed, is seated on a cloud surrounded by Victories". Her shield is ornamented with a portrait of Louis XIV. The coves contain the three conquered enemies (Germany, on her knees, with her eagle; Spain, threatening, with her roaring lion and Holland, lying on her lion, as well as Bellona, the goddess of war, raging with anger between Rebellion and Discord.

THE HALL OF MIRRORS

Originally, this was simply a terrace which Louis XIV had created above one section of the building erected by Le Vau when he came to enlarge the ground floor of Louis XIII's small château.

In 1678, the King decided to have a hall built to link the North and South apartments. The numerous teams of decorators worked under the direction of Le Brun from 1679 to 1689.

The Hall of Mirrors is lit from the gardens and the park by seventeen large arched windows offering a view that stretches away as far as the horizon. They are reflected in the bevelled mirrors of seventeen simulated arcades. The arches of the windows and arcades are ornamented with Louis XIV's emblem, the Rhodian sun, alternating with lion skins. Between the windows and the arcades stand twenty-four pilasters of red Rance marble, with gilt-bronze capitals. These were cast by Caffieri after sketches by Le Brun, whom Colbert had asked to create a "French order" for the occasion. This order consists of a *fleur-de-lis* surmounted by the royal sun and flanked by two Gallic cocks against a background of palm branches.

The Hall of Mirrors

Lamp bearers in the Hall of Mirrors

Towards the middle of the gallery, amidst the row of windows and arcades, four marble niches with trophies above them have been set into the walls. Louis XIV had the finest classical statues in his collection placed there. These were later moved to the Louvre, but some have been returned to their original places: in 1953, the "Versailles Bacchus", "Urania crowned with stars" and "Modesty" and, in 1975, "The modest Venus". Twelve busts of Roman emperors of marble and porphyry and several porphyry and alabaster vases complete the décor.

On the marble wall panels, particularly on either side of the bays opening on to the War and Peace Drawing Rooms, are gilt-bronze reliefs of trophies and weapons, the work of Coysevox, Tubi, Le Gros and Massou. Finally, the gilded stucco cornice is decorated with royal crowns and emblems of the orders of Saint Michael and the Holy Spirit.

The vaulted ceiling is entirely covered with paintings by Le Brun, some carried out with the help of artists from his studio. This is the largest pictorial ensemble in France. The story of Louis XIV, from the beginning of his personal reign in 1661 to the Peace of Nimeguen in 1678, is told there in classical allegorical

WAR DRAWING ROOM

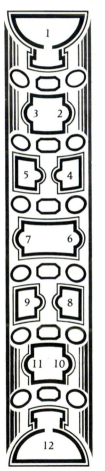

Themes of the nine large paintings on the ceiling from the War Drawing Room to the Peace Drawing Room:

1. *Alliance of Germany and Spain with Holland, 1672.*
2. *Crossing the Rhine in the presence of the enemy, 1672.*
3. *The King takes Maestricht in thirteen days, 1673*
4. *The King giving orders to attack four of Holland's strongholds at the same time, 1672.*
5. *The King arming his fleet and his army, 1672*
6. *The King governs alone, 1661.*
7. *Pomp of France's neighbouring powers.*
8. *Franche-Comté conquered a second time, 1674.*
9. *Resolution passed to make war on the Dutch, 1674.*
10. *Capture of the city and citadel of Ghent in six days, 1678.*
11. *Spanish action destroyed by the capture of Ghent.*
12. *Holland accepts peace and breaks with Germany and Spain, 1678.*

PEACE DRAWING ROOM

"The King governs alone"

"Crossing the Rhine"

style. The central painting portrays "Louis XIV governing alone": the King, in all the glow of youth, dressed in the style of Antiquity, his shoulders covered with an ermine-lined mantle, is seated on a stone throne; behind him, Glory shows him a crown of stars in the sky; France, recognizable by the *fleur-de-lis* on her mantle and shield, sits on his left; the Graces and Hymen evoke the King's recent marriage; at his feet little children play various games, while time, with his scythe and hourglass, holds a rich fabric over him.

This central work is surrounded by eight large paintings of the King's military victories. They were painted on canvas and then applied to the ceiling, while the twelve medallions and six monochrome paintings of civil reforms were executed directly on to the specially prepared surface of the ceiling.

The Hall of Mirrors was embellished with a sumptuous suite of silver furniture including orange-tree containers, tables and forty-one chandeliers and candlestands. This suite was melted down in 1689 and replaced by furniture of carved, gilded wood, consisting of tables, candlestands and stools.

The windows were provided with curtains of white damask with the

*A trophy
in bronze relief*

King's monogram embroidered in gold and on the floor lay two enormous Savonnerie carpets matching the colours on the ceiling.

The Hall of Mirrors was used above all as a passageway from the King's Apartments to those of the Queen. It enabled one to avoid the King's Bedchamber by going through the Bull's Eye Drawing Room or Council Chamber. Every day the courtiers would stand in attendance here as the King and the Royal Family went by on their way to and from mass.

But it was also used for receptions on exceptional occasions: the King granted a state audience to the Doge of Genoa in 1685, the Ambassadors of Siam in 1686, the Persian Ambassadors in 1715 and the Ambassador of Turkey in 1742. It was here, too, that all the illuminations were lit and masked balls were held on the occasion of marriages in the Royal Family. After the *Ancien Régime,* the Hall of Mirrors again became the setting for important events. On 18th January 1871, the King of Prussia solemnly accepted his crown as Emperor of Germany here.

The 28th June 1919 saw the signing of the Treaty of Versailles which put an end to the First World War.

The décor reconstituted today is that chosen to celebrate the marriage of the Dauphin to Marie-Antoinette in 1770; twenty-four candlestands (twelve with figures of women, by Babel, and twelve of children, by Folliot) were executed from original models in the Museum of Versailles. Twenty chandeliers of silvered bronze adorned with Bohemian crystal are a reminder of the lighting in the Hall of Mirrors for official festivities during the Ancien Régime.

*The Hall of Mirrors
towards the Peace Drawing Room*

THE QUEEN'S APARTMENT

The Queen's Apartment, its rooms overlooking the South Parterre, also called the Parterre of Flowers or Venus Parterre, is parallel to the King's State Apartment and was begun in 1671. After its completion in 1680, the décor was altered several times. During Louis XV's reign, the Peace Drawing Room, which had become the Queen's Games Room, was made part of the Queen's Apartment, which contains four other rooms: the Guard Room, which opens on to the marble stairway called the Queen's Staircase, the *Grand Couvert* antechamber, the Room of the Queen's Gentlemen and the Bedchamber. Today the apartment is, unfortunately, visited in reverse and not in the original, logical order.

THE PEACE DRAWING ROOM

Situated at the south end of the Hall of Mirrors, the Peace Drawing Room matches the War Drawing Room particularly by virtue of its décor of marble, mirrors and gilt-bronze. It became part of the Queen's Apartment in

1710, when the large archway leading to the Hall of Mirrors was closed off by means of a mobile partition.

The ceiling was painted by Le Brun. In the centre, one sees France crossing the skies in a chariot drawn by four doves, preceded by Peace crowned by Glory with the halo of Immortality and accompanied by Hymen (an allusion to the royal marriages which were one of the first results of the treaties), while Magnificence shows her the plans of buildings to be erected. On the coves "Spain", "Christian Europe at Peace", "Germany" and "Holland".

The large fireplace is very simply framed with a broad moulding of

The ceiling of the Peace Drawing Room

The Peace
Drawing Room

green marble. Set into the wall above it is a large oval painting, executed by Lemoine in 1729. It portrays "Louis XV bestowing peace on Europe" and shows the King at the age of nineteen holding out an olive branch to Europe. Piety and Fecundity present to him his two elder daughters, the twins Louise-Elisabeth and Anne-Henriette, born at Versailles on 14th August 1727. In the background, Discord attempts to open the door of the Temple of Janus, but Mercury is there to denounce her to Minerva.

In the fireplace, with its cast-iron plate bearing the arms of France and Navarra, are the magnificent gilt-bronze andirons in the form of two lions facing each other, created for this room by Boizot on Marie Antoinette's request.

The décor, like that of the War Drawing-Room, is completed by busts of Roman emperors with porphyry heads and marble drapery. In 1778, to entertain herself, Marie-Antoinette had a little theatre installed, with the back of the stage set against the archway of the great gallery.

This room was usually called the Queen's Games Room. On Sundays, Maria Leczinska held concerts of sacred or secular music here.

THE QUEEN'S BEDCHAMBER

This bedchamber was first occupied by Queen Marie-Thérèse, for whom the first décor was created from 1671 to 1689.

On the Dauphin's birth in 1729, it was decided to renew the décor for Maria Leczinska. Robert de Cotte designed the ornamentation, Verberckt, Dugoulon and Goupil executed the wainscoting and work was completed in 1735 by the Gabriels, father and son.

On the ceiling are four monochrome medallions, the work of Boucher. They depict Charity, Plenty, Fidelity and Prudence, four essentially feminine virtues characteristic of royalty. The overdoors, dated 1734, portray ''Youth and Virtue presenting the two princesses to France'', by Natoire, and ''Glory taking possession of the Children of France'', by Jean-François de Troy.

When Marie-Antoinette moved here in 1770, the sculptor, Antoine Rousseau, was commissioned to add to the arms of France and Navarra in the corners of the ceiling the two-headed eagle of the House of Austria.

Then, in 1773, the Queen had the Savonnerie tapestry portraits of her mother, Empress Maria-Theresa, her brother, Emperor Joseph II and her husband, Louis XVI, placed above the mirrors between the windows, over the fireplace and opposite it.

Finally, the original fireplace was replaced in 1782 by the one of Griotte marble with gilt bronzes here today.

The Queen's Bedchamber was the most important room in her Apartment. It was here that, each morning after her *toilette,* she would grant her private audiences.

Nineteen Children of France were born in this chamber.

The Queen's Bedchamber (1985)

This
exceptional
work of
reconstitution
would,
nevertheless,
have remained
incomplete
without the
balustrade
which was to
be found in
every royal
chamber. The
one which
stood here
in 1789
disappeared
during the
Revolution. It
dated from the
time of Maria
Leczinska and
was replaced
in 1975 by a
carved gilt
balustrade very
similar in
design to that
chosen by
Maria
Leczinska.

*The Queen's
Bedchamber*

*The Queen's
Bedchamber (1975)*

Here, too, two Queens and two Dauphines died : Marie-Thérèse of Austria in 1683 and Maria-Leczinska in 1768, and Maria Christina of Bavaria in 1690 and Marie-Adélaïde of Savoy in 1712. If a Queen died before the King, it was the custom to give this apartment to the Dauphine. It was connected to that of the Dauphin on the ground floor by means of an inner staircase.

Marie-Antoinette slept in this bedchamber from 1770 until the night of the 5th October 1789 when she was forced to flee the revolutionary mobs who had invaded the apartments.

The curtains and fabrics adorning the alcove bed and seats were this room's main decoration and were changed with the seasons.

Several years ago, when it was decided to restore the entire décor of this room which had been stripped bare, Marie-Antoinette's last summer wallhanging, delivered in 1787, was selected.

The original bedspread had been found and the Union of Silk Weavers of Lyons offered to weave and donate the alcove fabric of white brocaded Tours silk, embroidered with large bouquets of flowers in multi-coloured silk. Generous donations by the American friends of France made it possible to recreate the extremely sumptuous furnishings on the bed and to reweave the magnificent alcove carpet after a fragment of the original. To the left of the bed stands the jewelry cabinet by Schwerdfeger adorned with Sèvres porcelain and miniatures given to Marie-Antoinette by the city of Paris in 1787.

The andirons in the form of sphinxes and the gilt-bronze wall-clock which were here in Marie-Antoinette's time were returned in 1975 and the fireplace once again has its screen delivered by Sené in 1787 for the summer furnishings. Finally, two armchairs and eight folding stools covered in the same silk fabric complete the ensemble.

THE ROOM OF THE QUEEN'S GENTLEMEN

Originally, this room was used as an antechamber to Marie-Thérèse's apartment. It then became the Queen's Drawing Room and, later, the State Cabinet during the time of Maria Leczinska. Under Marie-Antoinette, the room once again became the Room of the Queen's Gentlemen.

All that remains of the former décor carried out under Le Brun for Queen Marie-Thérèse is the ceiling painted in 1671 by Michel Corneille. The themes chosen were the arts and sicences practised by celebrated female figures of Antiquity.

When Marie-Antoinette's second son, the Duc de Normandie, the future Louis XVII, was born in 1785, the Queen asked her architect, Mique, to redecorate the room entirely. The marble and stucco were replaced by waist-high wainscoting, and the walls were covered with hangings of apple-green silk, galooned with gold. Mirrors and a very fine slate-blue marble fireplace adorned with chased bronze by Gouthière completed the décor. Two paintings by J.B. Regnault which had been displayed at the 1785 Salon were hung above the doors: "Pygmalion on his knees besee-

The gilt-bronze
candelabra
once more stand
on the corner
cupboards for
which they
were intended.
Andirons
of the same
design as the
originals
represent cupids
warming their
hands before
a fire and
were delivered
in 1786.
The firescreen
made for
Louis XVI's
bedchamber at
Compiègne, a
late 18th century
chandelier,
folding stools
and a
splendid
Savonnerie
carpet from
the royal
collections
complete this
décor which
has now been
almost entirely
restored
as it was under
the Ancien
Régime.

*The Room
of the Queen's Gentlemen*

"Mercury spreading his influence over the Arts and Sciences"
ceiling by Michel Corneille

54

In the centre, "Mercury spreads his influence over the Arts and Sciences". The god is accompanied by Eloquence, Poetry, Geometry and other sciences he had invented. In the corners of the coves, Vigilance, Learning, Trade and Diligence frame paintings of "Sapho singing and playing the lyre", "Penelope weaving her tapestry", "Aspasia in discussion with the philosphers" and "Cerisene encouraging painting".

ching Venus to animate his statue" and "The Origins of Painting". The décor of this room was restored as it had been at the time of Marie-Antoinette.

Two chests of drawers and two corner cupboards executed by Riesener in 1786 were returned to the places along the walls for which they had originally been intended. They are of mahogany adorned with gilt-bronzes which match those of the fireplace : a frieze composed of waves of foliated scrollwork adorns the chimneypiece which is of slateblue marble, like the fireplace.

On the chest of drawers opposite the fireplace stood an 18th century porcelaine Ming vase with a gilded bronze setting from the collections of Marie-Antoinette. Above the other chest of drawers hangs a large tapestry portrait of Louis XV executed in 1770 by Cozette, after Van Loo.

It is accompanied by four paintings by François Boucher representing "Fishing", "Venus and Vulcan", "Neptune and Amymone" and the "Fortune-Teller".

On the chimney, two "ostrich" candelabras flanking a magnificent "camel" clock were originally in the Turkish bedroom of the Comte d'Artois.

"Queen Marie-Antoinette and her children"
by Elisabeth Vigée-Lebrun

In this famous painting, the Queen's favourite portraitist has shown her in the company of her three children. On the left, Madame Royale tenderly holds her mother's arm. On the right, the Dauphin, who to die in 1789, points to the empty cradle of his little sister, Madame Sophie-Béatrice, who was had died not long before. Finally, the Queen holds on her knee the Duc de Normandie, later to become Louis XVII.

THE GRAND COUVERT DINING ROOM

The name usually given to this room was the Queen's Antechamber, for it was here that the visitors who had come from the Room of the Queen's Guard would wait to be brought before Her Majesty, either in the Room of the Queen's Gentlemen or in her Bedchamber when she granted an audience or held her "circle".

The décor created for Queen Marie-Thérèse has remained unaltered. The lower part of the walls is lined with marble panels and a cornice with gilded consoles and small trophies runs along the top beneath the ceiling. In the corners are large gilded trophies surmounted with cupids.

The central ceiling painting, by Claude Vignon, has gone and been replaced by an old replica of "Darius' Tent", by Le Brun. However, several other paintings by Vignon still remain on the archings: "Rodogun at her *Toilette*", "Bellona burning Cybele's Face" and "Arpelia rescuing her husband"; there are also five works by Paillet: "Artemis on board Xerxes' Ships", "Fury and War", "Zenobia fighting against Emperor Aurelian", "Ipsicrates following her husband Mithridates to War" and "Clelia on horseback with her companions".

The overdoors are adorned with painted trophies and weapons by Madeleine de Boulogne which were displayed at the 1673 Salon. Along the walls, set out around a large Savonnerie carpet, are a number of benches and stools covered with old Gobelins tapestries.

This room is called the *Grand Couvert* Dining Room for it was here that the Queen ate in public, often in the company of the King. It was during one of these *Grands Couverts* that Mozart, at the age of seven, was presented to the King and Queen by his father, in the winter of 1764.

War Trophy
(ceiling corner)

As part of the restoration of this room which is at present underway, the two doors in the far wall have been returned here. Like the doors in the passage, they are surmounted by paintings by Madeleine de Boulogne which were exhibited at the 1673 Salon. The Languedoc marble fireplace with its pier glass commissioned by Marie-Antoinette has also been put in its original setting.
On the mantelpiece a replica of the "Ariadne Asleep" by Pierre Julien (1731-1804) has been placed.

The Queen's Antechamber

"Jupiter accompanied by Justice and Piety"
ceiling by Noël Coypel

THE ROOM
OF THE QUEEN'S GUARD

In 1672, this site was occupied by the galleries of the chapel, the altar being on the ground floor. When the chapel was transfered to the adjoining room (the Coronation Room), in 1676, a floor was laid and the walls covered with marble panels. This décor was completed in 1681. The overdoors are embellished with gilded metal bas-reliefs by Le Gros and Massou.

With its marble and paintings this room is one of the finest achievements of Le Brun's art.

The entire painted decoration of the room was executed by Noël Coypel. In an octagonal painting in the centre of the ceiling he has depicted Jupiter crossing the sky in his chariot, accompanied by two figures of Justice and Piety.

The Ruler of Olympus, holding his divine rod, stands on his silver chariot drawn by two eagles; on his left are two figures of Justice, one bearing an axe with a fasces, the other a cornucopia. A winged figure of Piety on the right casts an admiring look at the god. Around about, little genii wave flowers or, wielding their swords, hunt a centaur and other harmful creatures. These divine virtues are illustrated by the paintings in the

coves with examples from Antiquity. "Ptolemy Philadelphia granting the Jews their Freedom", "Alexander Severus having Corn distributed to the people", "Trajan dispensing Justice" and "Solon explaining his laws to the Athenians".

These five large compositions, painted by Noël Coypel, were originally intended for the King's State Cabinet or Jupiter Drawing-Room, situated on the site of the War Drawing Room.

A *trompe-l'œil* frieze has been painted in the corners of the ceiling. Courtisans in dress of the Louis XIV period lean over a simulated balustrade and seem to be observing the visitors with curiosity.

Two more paintings by Noël Coypel illustrate other aspects of the story of Jupiter on the walls: over the fireplace, a "Sacrifice to the Ruler of Olympus" and, on the opposite wall, "The Corybants dancing to prevent his cries from reaching Saturn".

Because of its location, people were constantly coming and going in this room where the Guards, all Gentlemen, were stationed to ensure the safety of the Queen. It was here that, on 6th October 1789, they did everything in their power to hold out against the invading mobs coming up the Queen's Staircase.

"Dance of the Corybants"
by Noël Coypel

THE CORONATION ROOM

This room, which continues the Queen's State Apartment, owes its name to the painting of the "Coronation of Napoleon I", by David, which Louis-Philippe had placed here. From 1676 to 1682, the third chapel had occupied the ground-floor and first floor; later, when a floor was laid, it become the Great Guard Room.

It was there that, each Holy Thursday, the ceremony commemorating the Last Supper took place. On this occasion, the King of France would wash the feet of thirteen childdren from poor families.

In order to provide a suitable setting for the two large paintings commissioned by Napoleon I in honour of his being crowned Emperor, "The Coronation" and "The Distribution of the Eagle Standards", Louis-Philippe had the ceiling of this room raised. On the wall opposite the windows hangs "The Battle of Aboukir", commissioned by Murat from Gros. The overdoors are embellished with figures of Courage, Genius, Generosity and Constance, the work of Gérard. Finally, an allegorical painting by Callet on the ceiling evokes the "18th Brummaire".

The painting of the coronation, which was moved to the Louvre for the 1889 Exhibition, was replaced in 1948 by a replica by David begun in 1808 and completed in exile in Brussels in 1821; the painter himself preferred it to the original.

The famous work depicts the historical moment when Napoleon I, who had just been crowned by Pope Pius VII, holds the crown over the head of Josephine kneeling before him. The painter has created perfect likenesses of all the dignitaries of the First Empire including Madame Mère, the Emperor's mother who, in fact, was not present at the ceremony.

Coronation of the Empress
by Jacques-Louis David

THE 1792 ROOM

The room which, today, is called the 1792 Room, was once used as a passage from the Great Guard Room, now the Coronation Room, to the Princes' Staircase and the South Wing. The Room of the Merchants under Louis XV, this room then became the Room of the Hundred Swiss Guards during the reign of Louis XVI. The paintings decorating it depict the 1792 campaign which ended in the victory of Valmy on 20th September.

THE HALL OF BATTLES

This Hall, 394 feet long and 43 feet wide, fills the entire length of the South Wing, at right angles to the Queen's Apartment.

Its creation was decided by King Louis-Philippe to replace the apartments which, during the 17th and 18th centuries, had been successively occupied by Monsieur, the Duc d'Orléans, Louis XIV's brother, and by his second wife, the Palatine Princess, as well as by the Duc and Duchesse de Chartres, the Duc d'Orléans, the Regent's son, by the Dauphin, the Comte d'Artois and Madame Elisabeth.

Under Louis-Philippe, this Hall was turned into a gallery of large paintings portraying the great military events of French History. Apart from several paintings already in existence, most of the works were especially commissioned. The architects, Fontaine and Nepveu, created an imposing décor for them. A wide cornice supports a coffered ceiling and the length of the hall is rythmed with Corinthian columns beneath the entablature.

Sixteen bronze plaques bear the names of the Princes, admirals, high dignitaries, marshals and great soldiers or generals killed or mortally wounded fighting for France.

The paintings cover fourteen centuries of French history, from the Battle of Tolbiac, fought by Clovis in 1496, to that of Wagram, which Napoleon won in 1809. The most remarkable works are "Bouvines" and "Fontenay", by Horace Vernet, "Saint Louis at Taillebourg", one of Delacroix's masterpieces, "Henri IV in Paris" and "Austerlitz", by Baron Gérard, and "The Capture of York Town", by Couder, in which one can recognize Washington between Rochambeau and La Fayette.

The Hall of Battles

Among the artists whose paintings hang in the Hall of Battles are Horace Vernet, Gérard, Couder, Larivière, the Scheffer Brothers, Steuben, Alaux, Heim, Dévéria etc... Delacroix is at their sides: in the "Battle of Taillebourg", the leader of the romantic movement in painting has represented "the moment when the King, Saint Louis, carried away by his fervour, crosses the Bridge over the Charente held by King Henry III's English army" on 21st July 1242.

"The Battle of Taillebourg"
by Delacroix

THE REVOLUTION, CONSULATE AND EMPIRE ROOMS

The south wing was built between 1678 and 1682 and was taken up by the Princes' Apartments under the *Ancien Régime*. In the 19th century it underwent major changes undertaken to transform the château into a history museum. The Hall of Battles was created on the first floor as mentioned above.

The ground floor consists of a series of thirteen rooms decorated with large paintings of the Napoleonic period framed by decorative panels which were commemorative works commissioned by Louis-Philippe. These rooms, dedicated to the campaigns of the Consulate and the Empire, were restored in 1978.

Thanks to work finished in 1986, part of the history museum is open to the public in a new setting on the attic storey, not only in the south wing and along the ceiling of the Hall of Battles, but also in the château's central building above the Queen's Apartments.

A stucco staircase built under Louis-Philippe leads to these rooms, where the visitor can follow the troubled times of the Revolution, the glorious moments of the Consulate and the Empire and the court splendors created by Napoleon I.

In fact it was often the same painters who witnessed the various phases of this turbulent period of French history, the main events of which barely cover twenty-five years (1789-1815).

*"The Cairo Uprising"
by Girodet*

THE MUSEUM OF HISTORY THE 19th CENTURY ROOMS

When Louis-Philippe changed Versailles into a museum, he had not only intended to reconcile the opposing political groups within his government born out of the revolution of 1830, but also to show all the military and civilian events making up the milestones of French history. In keeping with his idea, the Museum of the History of France stretches from the group of "neo-Gothic" rooms known as the Crusade Rooms (leading in to the Stone Gallery on the ground floor of the north wing) ending up in the attics of the same north wing with the period period from the Restoration of Louis XVIII in 1814 to World War I in 1914.

This century was marked by various attempts at governing, several revolutions and, finally, the triumph of the 3rd Republic. It is noticeable that the more painting and sculpture evolved, the less artists have been inclined, since the end of the last century, to faithfully portray either their contemporaries or the events they themselves witnessed.

In spite of this the Museum dedicated to France's glory will be presented with almost all its integrity.

Louis-Philippe and his sons,
by H. Vernet

THE QUEEN'S STAIRCASE

There has always been a staircase on this site. But the first, erected in 1672 and also of marble, was replaced by the larger one here today, built from 1679 to 1681.

The reconstruction was undertaken because the magnificent stairway leading to the King's Apartments had just been completed on the other side of the Courtyard and the Queen's Staircase therefore had to be fit to match it.

Marble of different colours is the basic decorative element; it has been used for the slabs, steps and balustrade of the staircase as well as the wall-panelling.

The overdoors are adorned with gilt-bronze bas-reliefs of two chimeras back to back and linked to a covered vase by a garland of oakleaves.

In a marble niche in the middle of the first floor landing, two cupids hold crossed quivers surmounted by a shield bearing the King's monogram: two inter-laced L's between olive-branches under the royal crown. Above it, two doves sitting on two intersecting torches and a crown of roses remind us that this staircase was that of the Queen.

In 1701, an arcade opening on to a vestibule with marble panelling, like that of the staircase, was set into the wall on the side of the Royal Courtyard. On the opposite wall, false perspectives with figures and flowers were painted to match the arcade.

This staircase, of which Félibien said that ''there is none other at Versailles as well known and as much used'', gave access to the Queen's Apartment and, via the Loggia, to the King's private suite overlooking the Marble Courtyard and overlooking Madame de Maintenon's apartment.

It was by means of this staircase that the crowd of Parisians managed to enter the château on 6th October 1789.

The Queen's
Staircase

MADAME DE MAINTENON'S APARTMENT

The loggia of the Queen's Staircase opens, to the right, on to a suite of rooms which Louis XIV had made into an apartment for his morganatic wife, Madame de Maintenon, who lived there until the sovereign's death in 1715. These rooms were then altered several times and, under Louis-Philippe, simply became part of the museum. A stairway leading to the attic storey made the antechambers smaller and took up part of the bedchamber. The layout of the rooms making up Madame de Maintenon's Apartment has been more or less recreated, with the exception of the bedchamber. Through lack of the silks and furniture which had decorated this apartment from the 17th century to the Revolution, 17th century furniture has been placed here, most of it coming from the Roudinesco donation. Furthermore, as an introduction to the tour of the Royal Apartments, paintings and sculptures have been gathered here in order to provide a better understanding of these rooms : preliminary drawings, some fairly elaborate sketches for the ceilings of the King's State Apartment as well as the Chapel, along with small

sculptures from the Crown Collections. Louis XIV was in the habit of coming to the apartment of the Marquise with one of his ministers to work on affairs of state. Finally, let us point out that it was in the State Cabinet that the royal family would gather around the monarch and Madame de Maintenon. It was here, too, that Racine produced "Athalie", with a cast of young ladies from the Institute of Saint-Cyr who were protected by the Great King's secret wife.

Madame de Maintenon's State Cabinet

THE KING'S APARTMENT

Unlike the State Apartment, the King's Apartment consisted of the rooms effectively lived in by the sovereign; it was there that the various daily ceremonies dictated by "etiquette" took place. After the loggia of the Queen's Staircase, one crosses two rooms which received their present painted décor in 1692: the guard room, its walls covered with simply moulded wainscoting, and the first antechamber or grand couvert antechamber (where the King, alone, ate his meals in public); this room contains paintings of battles (by Parrocel).

THE BULL'S EYE ANTECHAMBER

Until 1707, two rooms occupied this site: the King's first Bedchamber, with a window overlooking the Marble Courtyard, and a drawing room opening on to an inner Courtyard and called the Bassano Room.
When Louis XIV made the adjoining room his bedchamber, this drawing room was increased to its present size and a large bull's eye window, after which the room was named, set into the

specially raised ceiling. Right around the room, the sculptors Hardy, Poulletier, Poirier, Van Clève, Hutrelle and Flamen carved the remarkable cornice of "children at play".
Louis XIV had paintings by Vero-nese hung on the wainscoting. These were later replaced by portraits of royalty, the work of the Court painters, Mignard, Jean Nocret and François de Troy.
A large canvas by Jean Nocret depicts Louis XIV and his family in the guise of gods of Antiquity. Beneath stands a table with legs of carved, gilded wood and a top with a floral design of Florentine mosaic. Busts of Kings who had resided at Versailles were placed in this room: Louis XIV, by Coy-

The Bull's Eye
Drawing Room

68

sevox, Louis XV, by Gois and Louis XVI, by Houdon.

It was in this antechamber that the courtiers would wait each day behind the door leading to the King's Bedchamber until the time came to enter and attend the Private and State Rising Ceremonies and, in the evenings, the State and Private Retiring Ceremonies. Those who had the "royal warrant" were led in first by a Swiss guard, whose presence is called to mind by the halberd near the door.

THE KING'S BEDCHAMBER

It was not until 1701 that Louis XIV decided to make this his bedchamber. Prior to that, it had been the State Drawing Room of Louis XIII's small château and was lit by windows looking on to both the courtyard and the gardens, as the Hall of Mirrors did not exist before 1678. When the windows overlooking the gardens were removed, the whole décor was altered in 1679. Apart from the alcove created in 1701, the décor was the one we see here today. The gilded carving above the bed, representing "France watching over the King in his slumber", is the work of Coustou.

Louis XIV had his bedchamber adorned with fine paintings.

Louis XIV in his Bedchamber by Marot 69

After construction of the alcove, he had nine paintings by Valentin de Boulogne set into the attic between the ceiling and the cornice supported by Corinthian pilasters. Five of them remain today, "Saint Mark", "Saint Luke", "Saint Matthew", "Saint John" and "The Tribute to Caesar", to which was added "Agar in the desert", by Giovanni Lanfranco. The ornate frames above the doors still contain a portrait of François de Moncade, Marquis d'Aytona, and a self-portrait by Van Dyck. However, a "Saint John the Baptist", by Caravaggio, and a "Mary Magdalen" by Domenichino, were replaced by paintings of similar themes by Valentin and Guido Reni. In addition, but only in winter, the alcove contained "King David", by Domenichino, and "Saint John on Patmos", then attributed to Raphaël.

A bust of Louis XIV, by Coysevox, was placed on one of the two fireplaces.

It was in this room that, on 1st September 1715, he who had made his bedchamber the "sanctuary of Royalty" died.

After long years of effort the décor of this bedchamber has been totally reconstituted.

Looms of the time had to be used to reweave the bedspread, canopy and curtains around the bed as well as the wall-hangings in the alcove. (These were completed in 1980.) The latter consist of five silk panels with a crimson background, with gold brocade in large, stylized designs of flowers and foliage, in the purest 17th century tradition. These panels are separated by six Corinthian pilasters decorated with garlands of vine-leaves echoing the pilasters on the wall-panelling. This extremely sumptuous fabric embroidered in gold was also used for the two armchairs placed on either side of the bed. Thus, the décor of the room which, it may be said without exaggeration, was the very heart of France for three reigns, has been restored.

The Bedchamber seen from the royal alcove

The King's Bedchamber

THE COUNCIL CHAMBER

This site was formerly occupied by two rooms: the King's Cabinet, where he held his various councils with his Ministers, and the Cabinet of Terms, also called the Cabinet of Periwigs because the King's wigs, which he changed several times daily, were kept in a wardrobe here.

In 1775, Louis XV ordered his architect, Ange-Jacques Gabriel, to make the two rooms into one, larger by about 8 feet gained on the Courtyard of the Stags side. Gabriel also designed the wainscoting which was carved by Antoine Rousseau. Each panel illustrates one of the King's councils: Peace, War and the Navy, symbolized by children playing (a perfect example of the rococo style).

Under the *Ancien Régime,* the overdoors were embellished with paintings: "The separation of Saint Peter and Saint Paul", by Lanfranco, and, by Nicolas Poussin, a "Bacchante", "Pyrrhus saved" and "The Blind of Jericho". These paintings have been replaced by works belonging to the royal collections: "Jupiter ordering Mercury to rescue Io" and "The Birth of Minerva" (on the King's Bedchamber side), "Minerva on Parnassus" and

*Bust of Alexander the Great
with its gilt-bronze drapery*

"Minerva and Neptune arguing as to who should name the city of Athens", (the last three paintings are by Houasse).

The bust of Alexander, with its gilt-bronze drapery by Girardon, and that of Scipio, its drapery by Coustou now restored, were returned to this room in 1975.

The Council Chamber played a decisive role in the life of the King and of his Court. The ministerial council was held here each morning and it was here that all the important decisions of the reigns of Louis XV and Louis XVI were made. The King also granted private audiences here and received all the members of Court who came before to present their congratulations or condolences, as the occasion demanded.

The Council Table has been restored in its former dimensions and covered with a sumptuous fabric of embroidered blue satin rewoven at Lyons after a sample of the one executed for Louis XV. The same fabric covers the two Louis XV stools of carved, gilded wood and was used for the large curtains.

On the reddish marble fireplace with gilt-bronze ornamentation stands a gilt-bronze clock made in 1754 for Louis XV. The medallion with the King's profile is held by one of the putti which decorate this magnificent room.

THE KING'S PRIVATE APARTMENT

During the reign of Louis XIV, the King's private apartment consisted of a series of drawing rooms and cabinets which, with the exception of the billiards room, formed a veritable private museum. Only rare guests of honour, scholars and artists were admitted to contemplate the masterpieces it contained.

In 1738, when Louis XV had a small bedchamber created for himself here, the private apartment was reorganized to include a first antechamber (Cabinet of the Dogs), second antechamber (Clock Cabinet) and study (Private Cabinet). Despite the alterations which were made during the 18th century, this apartment continued to be used as the private suite intended by Louis XV until the end of Louis XVI's reign.

LOUIS XV's BEDCHAMBER

Originally, this room was smaller and, besides the two windows overlooking the Marble Courtyard, had two more looking on to the Courtyard of the Stags.

Louis XV's Bedchamber

Chimneypiece in Louis XV's Bedchamber

It was first used as a billiards room by Louis XIV, then as the Cabinet of the Dogs, where the King fed his favourite animals.

Louis XV decided to make this his bedchamber in 1738. An alcove was therefore added on the Courtyard of the Stags side. The architect Gabriel designed the wood panelling carved by Verberckt which surrounds the fine fireplace of Serancolin marble. Paintings by great artists were set over the doors. In their place are four portraits of Louis XV's daughters.

The room was sumptuously furnished. Magnificent fabrics, altered according to the seasons, were used for the bed, the two armchairs, the eight folding stools, the fire screen, the folding screen, the doors and the windows. Two large regulator clocks stood on either side of the alcove and, on a chest of drawers opposite the fireplace, were placed the finest pieces in the royal gold plate.

Louis XV, who only used Louis XIV's Bedchamber for the State Rising and Retiring Ceremonies, always slept in this chamber. He died here on 10th May 1774, on a camp bed placed in the centre of the room.

The summer alcove tapestry is now being rewoven in gold brocaded Tours silk with a flower motif cover, delivered in 1785. To the far left opens a door leading to the Dressing Room with its wainscoting altered in 1788 for Louis XVI.

THE CLOCK CABINET

The two rooms originally here were made into one in 1738. The famous astronomical clock to which the room owes its name was placed on a marble base set into the floor in 1760.

This clock was designed by Passement, fitted with a mechanism by Dauthiau and decorated with

The Clock
Cabinet

The Cabinet of the Dogs, in fact the first antechamber of the King's Private Apartment, was created in 1738 on the site of a staircase. To decorate it, Gabriel used the wainscoting previously in Louis XIV's former billiards room (the present Bedchamber of Louis XV). Its name comes from the kennels placed along the walls for Louis XV's favourite dogs. The After-Hunt Dining Room belonged to the King's Cabinets and not to his private suite. It was created in 1750 on the site of Louis XV's former bathroom. It was in this dining room that Louis XV would invite some of the people who had taken part in the hunt to dine with him.

THE KING'S PRIVATE CABINET

It was only in 1753 that this room became the King's Study. Prior to that it had been Louis XIV's Billiards Rooms and then his Picture Gallery; at that time it was connected to the adjoining rooms by two arcades. In 1738, Louis XV had the arcades removed and a fireplace of Italian griotte marble erected. At the same time, he commissioned the cabinet-maker

gilt bronzes by Caffieri. It was presented to the *Académie des Sciences* in 1749 and to the King in 1753. In the crystal globe on the top the planets revolve around the sun according to the Copernican system.

In the centre of the room is a copy by Vassé of the equestrian statue of Louis XV by Bouchardon which, until its destruction in 1792, had stood in the *Place Louis XV* in Paris, today the *Place de la Concorde*. In 1774, Foliot delivered twenty-four gilded chairs for this and the following room. Only six were found again and are displayed in the private cabinet.

The furnishings are completed by a carved, gilt-wood barometer by Lemaire, delivered in 1774, and four gilt-wood rococo tables whose tops depict the royal hunts in the forests of Versailles, Fontainebleau and Saint-Germain.

Gaudreaux to make a medal-chest in the form of a chest of drawers decorated with magnificent gilt-bronzes.

In 1753, the walls were lined with wainscoting designed by Gabriel and carved by Verberckt. The cabinet-maker Joubert delivered two corner cupboards to match the medal chest in 1755 and, in 1760, Louis XV commissioned from Oeben the famous roll-top writing desk in the centre of the room. It had to be completed in 1769 by Riesener, who had married Oeben's widow.

This remarkable piece of furniture may be entirely locked by a single mechanism; only the small drawers containing the ink-wells remained open for the "King's attendants" to fill. The writing desk was returned to Versailles from the Louvre in 1957.

Louis XVI had three extraordinary objects placed in this room, all masterpieces executed by the bronze-smith Thomire in 1785: the two Sèvres porcelain vases and the famous "American Independence candelabrum". Recently, the crimson Genoan velvet damask galantined with gold was rewoven for the curtains and the six chairs by Foliot which were brought back from Fontainebleau in 1957. This room is now one of the finest and most completely restored in the château.

THE NEW ROOMS

This is a suite of rooms which Louis XV had created on the site of a *Small Gallery* constructed in 1684 to replace Madame de Montespan's apartment. It had five windows looking on to the Royal Courtyard and a drawing-room at each end, the same size as the present Cabinet of the Gold Plate. The ceilings were painted by Mignard. In 1752, the whole suite was destroyed to make room for an apartment for Louis XV's daughter, Madame Adélaïde, whom he wished to have near him. The Princess lived here until 1769, when the rooms which had made up her apartment were integrated into the King's private suite and called the "New Rooms".

MADAME ADELAIDE'S MUSIC ROOM

This room became the Music Room of Madame Adélaïde, Louis XV's daughter, in the apartment he had created for her in 1752. The wood-panelling installed in 1767 was carved after designs by Gabriel and is decorated with wonderful musical trophies which are undoubtedly among the finest in the Louis XV style.

It was here that the young Mozart played before the Royal Family in the winter of 1763-1764.

A small room beyond served as Louis XV's bathroom, for which the wainscoting, with its gilding of green, mat, burnished and bronze hues, was executed. Louis XVI made this his *Très-Arrière-Cabinet* or Room of the Privy Purse, where he kept the records of his private accounts. One enters by means of a small corridor constructed in the 19th century.

Madame Adélaïde's Music Room

78

LOUIS XVI'S LIBRARY

Upon his accession to the throne in 1774, Louis XVI entrusted Gabriel with the task of designing the wainscoting created by Antoine Rousseau. Above the mirrors are medallions portraying Apollo, the Arts and France holding the King's portrait. The bookcases, including the two entrance doors with their simulated book-bindings, are embellished in the curved corners of the room with trophies symbolizing the various literary forms. The marble and bronzes of the fireplace were carved by Boizot and Thomire respectively; it was executed for Madame Du Barry at Fontainebleau and is decorated with two angels bearing baskets. This library is also furnished with a roll-top desk by Roentgen and a chest of drawers made by Benneman in 1787. Also part of the original furniture are the terrestrial globe and the round table by Riesener whose top consists of a single piece of mahogany.

Placed around the room are seats by Séné commissioned for one of Louis XVI's drawing-rooms at Compiègne. They have been reupholstered with their original "painted Pekin" fabric. That used for the curtains and screen is also identical to the one chosen by Louis XVI for this room.

Louis XVI's Library

79

THE DINING ROOM OF THE NEW ROOMS

The last drawing-room in the Small Gallery and then Madame Adélaïde's State Cabinet (1752 to 1769), this room was later used as a dining-room by Louis XV. During Louis XVI's reign it was also called the Porcelain Dining Room (each year at Christmas the latest pieces produced by the Sèvres Manufactury were exhibited here).

On the white painted wainscoting were hung porcelain plates depic-

*Royal Hunts
in the Porcelain Dining Room*

ting the Royal Hunts, based on the tapestries woven under Louis XV after Oudry's sketches. On these plaques, the figure of Louis XV was simply replaced by that of his grandson.

Further along, a room disfigured in the 19th century still has one of the doors which led from the former Ambassadors' Staircase to the Venus Drawing Room.

LOUIS XVI'S GAMES ROOM

Louis XVI's Games Room was created in 1775. It had previously been Louis XIV's Cabinet of Curios and Rare Objects and then Madame Adélaïde's first antechamber. The wainscoting was altered but the chimney, which was removed during the 19th century, has been reinstalled. This room contains most of its original furniture and its former splendour has been restored particularly due to the four corner cupboards by Riesener and nineteen chairs by Boulard. The crimson and gold damask was rewoven at Lyons for the chairs and curtains. On the wood panelling hang the ten gouaches by Van Blarenberghe portraying important military events of Louis XV's reign.

MARIE-ANTOINETTE'S CABINETS

The Queen's Private Cabinets, situated behind the State Apartments and overlooking an inner courtyard, served varying purposes under each Queen: Marie-Thérèse of Austria had an oratory created, Maria Leczinska liked to withdraw there to paint, embroider or talk in peace, whereas Marie-Antoinette would receive her gayer, livelier close friends or have the latest frivolous fashions which she loved shown to her.

These Cabinets, today as they were left by Marie-Antoinette, comprise essentially a bathroom and its retiring chamber, two libraries, a drawing room and a room called the Meridian Cabinet.

The Meridian Cabinet was named after the Queen's rest period in the middle of the day.

It is situated behind the Queen's Bedchamber in the State Apartments.

Formerly, the Duchesse de Bourgogne had an oratory here, then it became a small drawing room for Maria Leczinska and, finally, a staircase.

The present décor was created on the birth of the first Dauphin in 1781. The room is octagonal in shape, with a mirror-lined alcove opposite the window. In this refined décor it is difficult to distinguish the gilt bronzes framing the mirrors from the gilded wood carving of the wainscoting. The former represent eagles between Hercules' club and Omphales' mirror and the latter peacocks flanked by swords and distaffs.

The room is filled with symbols of the marital love uniting the two sovereigns: rose-tree branches, garlands of flowers, dolphins surrounded by lilies and hearts pierced with arrows. In 1955, the room was restored to its 1781 state. A blue damask with pomegranate seedlings and silver trimmings was used for the windows, the alcove and the settee and eight chairs by Jacob.

The décor is completed by a gilded, wooden console table made in 1781 for the Dauphin's birth (it bears his crown and heraldic animal), a table with a petrified wood top on a bronze and steel

The Meridian Cabinet

stand given to Marie-Antoinette by her sister, the Archiduchesse Marie-Anne, and various other objets d'art.

The Queen's Private Cabinet, or Gilded Drawing Room, which had previously been used as a drawing-room by Maria Leczinska, was entirely redecorated in 1783 in the style of Antiquity. The Queen's architect, Mique, designed the wood panelling carved by the Rousseau brothers; it depicts sphinxes back to back against an incense burner on a tripod. The red griotte marble fireplace is embellished with gilt-bronzes and figures of female caryatids.

Opposite the windows is an alcove lined with mirrors.

Marie-Antoinette's furniture has been scattered or lost. However, it has been replaced by other pieces equal in quality: a set of seats from the Queen's State Drawing Room in the Tuileries, a chest of drawers by Riesener which had been in the room of the Comtesse d'Artois' Gentlemen at Versailles, a pair of corner cupboards, two work tables, one of which is signed by Roentgen, a very rare harp, by Naderman, and various objets d'art.

A bust of Marie-Antoinette, by Boizot, keeps alive the Queen's presence in her Drawing Room.

On the mezzanine above the Queen's Private Cabinet small rooms including a billiards room, dining room and chambermaid's quarters have been restored as they stood before the Revolution. Here the Queen carried on with her private life, and it is even claimed that Fersen lived here.

The Queen's Private Cabinet

THE KING'S STAIRWAY

The King's Private Cabinets are reached by means of a staircase which was permanently erected here in 1754 and extended as far as the second floor in 1763.

*The King's
Stairway*

THE KING'S PRIVATE CABINETS AND MADAME DU BARRY'S APARTMENT

Situated on different levels under the château's roofs, directly above the King's apartments, this delightful suite of small rooms full of grace and

*Madame du Barry's
Library*

unexpected charm has dormer windows overlooking the Marble Courtyard and smaller ones looking on to inner courtyards. The talent of their decorators played an important part in concealing their rather thankless proportions by means of perfectly harmonious wainscoting.

These rooms were originally allocated to the King's courtiers and servants, such as Lazur, Louis XV's cook. Later, as these rooms could be easily reached from his apartment by means of inner stairways, Louis XV found it convenient to convert them into rooms arranged for his relaxation (library, physics and chemistry cabinets, aviaries, a bathroom, small dining-room...) and also to have an apartment created there for his latest mistress, from Madame de Mailly up to the last, Madame Du Barry.

After Louis XV's death, the virtuous Louis XVI banished Madame Du Barry from Court and gave her apartment to the Duc de Villequier, to Maurepas and others, keeping for himself a geography and joinery cabinet.

One should draw attention to the skill with which the architect has succeeded in disguising the sloping roof by means of deep window recesses, particularly in the Corner Cabinet. The delicately painted and gilded wainscoting has been restored to its former freshness in recent years.

One of the most delightful rooms in the château is the Library. First decorated for Madame Adélaïde, one of Louis XV's daughters, it was later given to Madame Du Barry.

In 1956, a gilded wood settee was placed in the mirror-lined alcove. Its basket-like shape is similar to that of Madame Du Barry's furniture and the settee which must have stood here then.

A chair from Madame Du Barry's time and a birdcage bearing her arms and adorned with Dresden china flowers are the only other pieces necessary to furnish this exquisite room.

The Apartment
of Madame du Barry

The curtain
with the arms of France

THE THEATRE

Ever since the first important buildings were erected under Louis XIV, temporary theatres had been built on various sites. In 1685, a project begun by the Italian stage-setter Vigarani (on the site of the present theatre at the end of the North Wing), was interrupted by the wars which marked the end of Louis XIV's reign. In 1700, a temprary theatre, which could be turned into a ballroom, was created in the vestibule of the Prince's Courtyard. Another theatre was created at the time of Madame de Pompadour, first in the Small Gallery and later in the Ambassadors' Staircase.

Finally, great festivities were held in the grounds of the Great Stables.

It was in 1748 that Louis XV decided to provide the château with a theatre worthy of it and commissioned his Head Architect, Ange-Jacques Gabriel, to elaborate the plans. Gabriel worked for twenty years on its constructions, continually altering and improving his plans. The foundations were laid but work on the project was brought to a halt by the Seven Years' War.

Gabriel was on the point of giving up when Louis XV suddenly ordered the building to be completed in twenty-one months for the marriage of his grandson, the Dauphin and future Louis XVI, to the Archduchesse Marie-Antoinette of Austria. The theatre was intended not only for operas but also for concerts, balls and banquets.

Gabriel designed an elliptical ground-plan and for acoustic as well as financial reasons, the theatre was built entirely of wood.

With the help of the stagesetter Arnoult, who advised him on the design of the stage (the largest in France after that of the Paris Opera), Gabriel created a décor of solid wood with boxes and tiers matching those in the theatre itself.

The Royal
Box

By means of winches, the floor of the theatre could be raised to the same level as the stage and, by covering the orchestra pit, a huge oval hall could be formed. When the partitions and benches in the boxes were removed, one could walk around the whole colonnade.

The marriage celebrations were held there on 16th and 17th May, 1770, with a performance of "Perseus", by Lully and Quinault, a full-dress ball, "Athalie" played by Mademoiselle Clairon, "Castor and Pollux" by Rameau, Voltaire's "Tancrede" and a dramatic ballet using magical stage-effects, "The Enchanted Tower". Similar festivities took place the following year for the marriages of the Comte de Provence, the Comte d'Artois and Madame Clothilde. The banquet for the officers of the King's Bodyguard in 1789 brought the celebrations held under the *Ancien Régime* to a riotous close.

During the Revolution, every possible article was sold: mirrors, wall-hangings, chandeliers, benches, etc. The theatre was used as the meeting-place for the people's society, "The Virtue of the *Sans-Culottes* of Versailles", before being closed down altogether.

It was not reopened until the inaugural celebrations were held for Louis XV's Museum. Restoration work undertaken on this occasion considerably altered the décor of the theatre. In 1871, the National Assembly sat there and later, from 1876 to 1879, the Senate. The ceiling canvas, painted by Durameau, was rolled up and stored behind the stage and replaced by a skylight supported by a metal framework which caused serious damage because of its weight. The theatre was about to fall into ruin when exemplary restoration work carried out between 1952 and 1957 endowed it with its former décor of blue and pink and its great azure curtain adorned with *fleurs-de-lis* and the royal arms embroidered in gold.

The Opera House
with painted set of the enlarged stage

This famous painting reveals the development in the 18th century of the taste for masked festivities and elegant disguises The Marquis de Sourches, Grand Provost of France, that is, Chief of Police, did not hesitate to appear as a musician with his wife and children in this "Pastoral Concert", painted by Drouais. The composition conjures up the luxury and gentleness of a refined civilization which lived in harmony with an idealized form of nature.

"The Pastoral Concert"
painted by Drouais

THE GROUND FLOOR OF THE CENTRAL BUILDING

In the first phase of the museum's reorganization paintings concerning the 18th century had been displayed in this part of the château. Since then further steps have been taken to reconstitute the apartments of the Children of France under Louis XV and Louis XVI. The apartments of the Dauphin, the son of Louis XV, and the Dauphine Maria Josepha of Saxony have been recreated on the south side.

However, the Guard Room and the first antechamber look out on to the Marble Courtyard.

Furthermore, there are small rooms behind the Dauphine's Apartment which were created under Louis XVIII for the Duchess of Angoulème and whose name they are still known by. To the north of the Lower Gallery (rebuilt as it stood under Louis XIV) the Apartments of Madame Adelaïde and Madame Victoire have also been recreated. The rearrangement of their library and private cabinets led to the coffering of the columns in the vestibule of the Bathing Apartment which had been uncovered during construction work commissioned by Louis-Philippe.

GROUND FLOOR OF THE CENTRAL BUILDING

THE DAUPHINE'S APARTMENT
1. 1st Antechamber (42)
2. 2nd Antechamber (43)
3. State Cabinet (44)
4. Bedchamber (45)
5. Private Cabinet (46)
6. Annex or *Arrière-Cabinets* Duchess of Angoulême

THE DAUPHIN'S APARTMENT
7. Library (47)
8. State Cabinet (48)
9. Bedchamber (49)
10. The Annex or *Arrière-Cabinets*
11. 2nd Antechamber (50)
12. LOWER GALLERY (51)

MADAME VICTOIRE'S APARTMENT
13. 1st Antechamber (52)
14. *Salon des Nobles* (53)
15. State Cabinet (54)
16. Bedchamber (55)
17. Private Cabinet (56a)
18. Library (56b)

a Leading to the Gardens
b Queen's Courtyard
c Dauphin's Courtyard
d Courtyard of the Stags
e King's private courtyard
f Louis-Philippe Staircase
g Paths leading to the Gardens

MADAME ADELAIDE'S APARTMENT
19. Private Cabinet (56c)
20. Bedchamber (57)
21. State Cabinet (58)
22. Archers' room
23. Vestibule of the Ambassadors' Stairway (26)
24. Vestibule (27b)
25. King's Guard Room (27a)
26. King's Stairway

THE CAPTAIN OF THE GUARDS' APARTMENT
27. State Cabinet (28)
28. Private Cabinet (28)
29. Bedchamber (29)

MARIE-ANTOINETTE'S APARTMENT
30. (Room 30)
31. The Queen's Bedchamber (31)
32. *Central Vestibule* (32)
33. Bathchamber (33b)

ENTRANCE ROOMS TO THE DAUPHIN'S APARTMENT
34. 1st Antechamber (33a)
35. Guard Room (34)

LOCATION OF THE KING'S DRESSING ROOM
36. (Rooms 35, 36, 37)
37. THE QUEEN'S STAIRCASE
38. Vestibule (38)

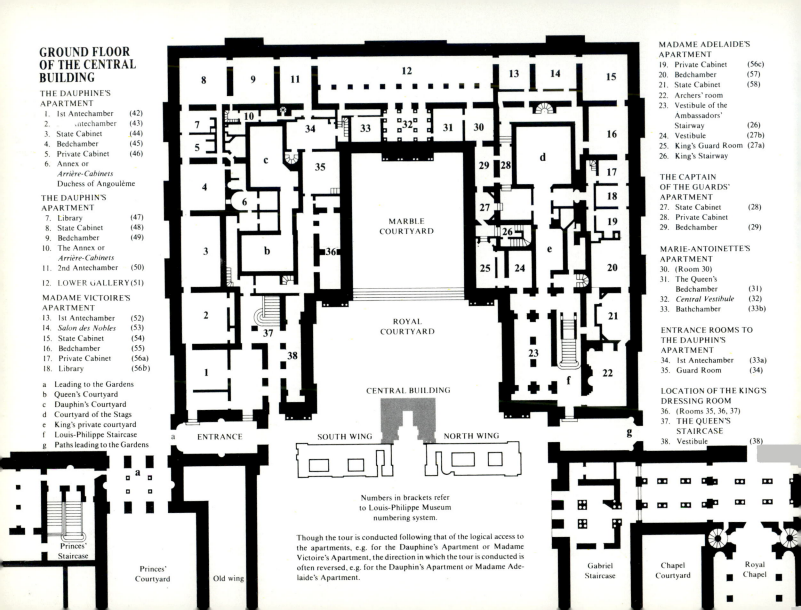

MARBLE COURTYARD

ROYAL COURTYARD

CENTRAL BUILDING

SOUTH WING   NORTH WING

ENTRANCE

Princes' Staircase

Princes' Courtyard   Old wing

Gabriel Staircase   Chapel Courtyard   Royal Chapel

Numbers in brackets refer to Louis-Philippe Museum numbering system.

Though the tour is conducted following that of the logical access to the apartments, e.g. for the Dauphine's Apartment or Madame Victoire's Apartment, the direction in which the tour is conducted is often reversed, e.g. for the Dauphin's Apartment or Madame Adelaide's Apartment.

*Felling the trees in the gardens of Versailles,
by Hubert-Robert (1775)*

Following the relevelling of the Marble Courtyard, the Guard Room of the King's Stairway, the Apartment of the Captain of the Guards and two rooms of Marie-Antoinette's Private Apartment on the ground floor flanking the Central Vestibule (bedchamber and bathchamber) have been re-established on the side of the Royal Courtyard.

Needless to say all this restoration work has been carried out either with the original remaining wainscoting or that kept in storage, identical copies or, when these could not be created, simple panelling.

The hangings are as similar as possible to those described in Ancien Régime inventories. As for the furniture, the original pieces have unfortunately not always been found and efforts have been made to gather as much as possible sets from former royal homes.

Be that as it may, most important is the iconography : the Regency and the reigns of Louis XV and Louis XVI are depicted in paintings and busts, some very fine in quality, and the numerous portraits by Nattier, Van Loo and Vigée-Lebrun should be mentionel.

Thus the visitor will be able to picture life at court in the 18th century and relive its main events.

GENERAL PLAN OF GARDENS

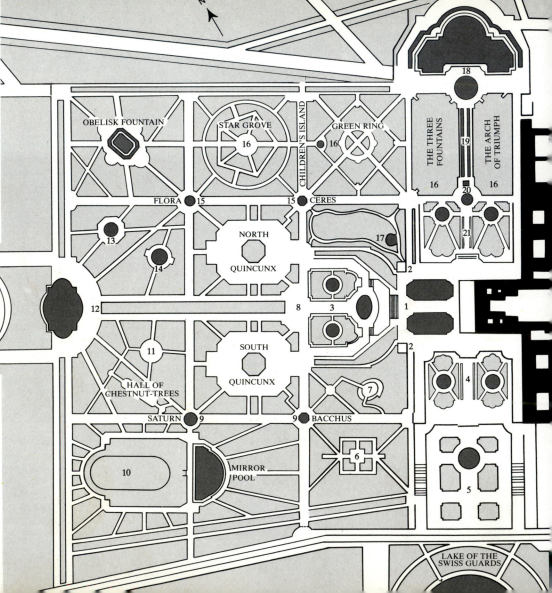

THE GARDENS

Versailles is the place of triumph for the gardens "à la française" with their rigorously ordered parterres where nature has been completely subjugated by an architect-gardener.

The park of Versailles, planned during the reign of Louis XIII, reached perfection under Louis XIV thanks to Le Nôtre, Le Brun and Jules Hardouin-Mansart.

Reduced in size at the end of the *Ancien Régime,* the park today covers an area of 2013 acres.

The park was designed by the gardener, André Le Nôtre, who worked at Vaux-le-Vicomte for Fouquet until the latter fell into disgrace. He then came to Versailles, where he laid out the great axes planned by Louis XIII's gardeners, extended the panoramas, increased the number of observation points and modelled the uneven, marshy ground of the estate into wide terraces leading from the château in three directions towards magnificent expanses of water: to the north, the Fountain of Neptune, to the west, the Grand Canal and, to the south, the Lake of the Swiss Guards.

Within the great axes run avenues intersecting at right angles to form one or two groves created by the inventive genius of Le Nôtre. Mansart, named Head Architect in 1686, collaborated with Le Nôtre in decorating the groves, naturally underlining the architectural aspect.

To these two creators of the Gardens of Versailles and Trianon a third must be added, Charles Le

The Parterre of Latona
a copy of a classical vase

A Nymph and a Cupid
by Magnier

Brun, Head Painter to the King, who, from 1664 onwards, designed most of the statues, vases and fountains decorating the park.

Their execution was entrusted to the most uncontestable talents of the time: Coysevox, Girardon, the Marsy brothers, Desjardins, Tuby, Le Hongre, etc. The sandy pathways were lined with fifteen to twenty foot high hedges and palisades into which niches were set for vases and statues. The trees, mostly yews, were pruned into various shapes: balls, pyramids and arcades.

Even in our day, one cannot help being astonished at the number of plants needed to decorate the two large parterres, the South Parterre and the Orangery Parterre: 150,000 in all. The flowers, kept blooming freshly and varied in species through the loving care of the gardeners and botanists, were one of the most admired luxuries of Versailles in the 17th century.

One of the great problems raised by the creation of the Versailles gardens was the water supply. Louis XIV first called in two Florentine engineers, the Francini brothers, who installed a pump on the banks of the pond at Clagny. The Marly machine, built by Arnold Deville and Rennequin Sualem from 1681 to 1684, carried the water from the Seine to Versailles via the Marly aqueduct. An attempt was even made to deviate the course of the Eure River. However, this project was interrupted by the war of 1688.

One cannot talk about the park of Versailles without mentioning the festivities which took place there. The daily walks taken there by the King, on foot or in a sedan-chair on wheels, in the company of his Court or important visitors, became the opportunity to hold concerts, light meals or fireworks in the various groves. Later, the festivities held by Louis XV no doubt matched the legendary splendour of Louis XIV's great celebrations.

*The château and the gardens
the North Parterre* 95

Under Louis XV, the hedges, which had been badly damaged during the terrible winter of 1709, were removed altogether. With them disappeared one of the most characteristic elements of Louis XIV's gardens which were not only destroyed by the effect of the bad weather. During the 18th century, when these gardens were left open to the public, the groves and statues were ruined by acts of vandalism and Louis XV was even forced to limit their access to his courtiers. On Louis XVI's accession to the throne, the entire park was replanted. Hubert Robert's paintings (see p. 94) are a reminder of this task. Several of the groves were completely transformed at this time. Finally, Louis XVIII had the lane of the Royal Island drained and a garden in the English style designed in front of the Mirror Fountain.

Nevertheless, the park as it is today still resembles that of Louis XIV fairly closely in its general lay-out. The King himself, in around 1705, wrote a short treatise called "The Manner of Presenting the Gardens of Versailles" in which the observation points and spots mostly likely to arouse the visitor's admiration are carefully indicated. With some exceptions, this will be the itinerary we shall follow.

The North Pond of the Water Parterre
Children at Play by Granier

The "instructions in the King's hand for a tour of the gardens" exists in several versions. The itinerary chosen here is the one called The Manner of presenting the Gardens of Versailles, "order to be followed" in twenty-five paragraphs, published in 1889 in the Revue de l'Histoire de Versailles. "After leaving the château by the vestibule of the Marble Courtyard, one goes on to the terrace. One should stop at the top of the stairway to take in the layout of the parterres, pools and fountains". Louis XIV.

The west façade seen from the Fountain of Diana

1 - THE WATER PARTERRE

The Water Parterre is a continuation of the magnificent château façade reconstructed by Jules Hardouin-Mansart in 1680. Only a terrace three steps higher separates the façade from the parterre which overlooks almost the whole park and from where the visitor may take in the various horizons of Versailles.

This parterre was not immediately given its final form as we know it today. The changes it underwent over the years can be divided into four essential phases. When Philibert Le Roy built the first château of Versailles in 1631, during the reign of Louis XIII, the King's Gardeners, Jacques Boyceau and Jacques de Menours, designed for this site a parterre consisting of arabesque-shaped flower-beds surrounding a small round pool. This was how the parterre, no doubt created before 1638, looked when Louis XIV visited Versailles in his youth.

However, the young King was not at all pleased with the appearance of the parterre as, in 1664 or 1668, the four squares of floral embroidery were replaced by two large, irregularly shaped lawns separated by a small path with a round pool at the end.

The War Vase
by Coysevox

The second design was changed between 1671 and 1674 when this section of the Park was called the Water Parterre. The lawns scattered with flowers disappeared and were replaced by an original, quadrilobate lawn whose main decorative element was the fountain. The Water Parterre then consisted of a round central pool with four others of irregular shape linked to it. There were two smaller ponds on the right and left.

It was then that Colbert ordered Le Brun to carry out the ''Great Commission of 1674'' which included what was to be the carved ornamentation of the Water Parterre: four ''Rapes'' (the only one executed, ''The Rape of Persephone by Pluto'', carved by Girardon, was later placed in the centre of the Colonnade) and twenty-four statues representing the four Elements, the four Parts, of the Day, the four Parts of the Earth, the four Seasons, the four types of Poetry and the four Temperaments. The finest sculptors worked on this commission, drawing their inspiration from sketches made by the painter, Le Brun. Before 1686, most were placed in the spots where we see them today, near the Fountains of the Animals, at the top of the Parterre of Latona and along the palisades of the North Parterre.

Four bronze
statues stand
on pedestals,
their backs to
the façade of
the central buildings.
They were cast
after classical
models by the
Keller brothers
and represent
Bacchus, Apollo,
Mercury and
Silenus. These
statues form a link
between the
décor of the
Water Parterre and
that of the
façade, whose
three front sections
are surmounted
with statues
of the twelve
months of the
year flanking
Apollo and
Diana. In the
corners of the
terrace stand
two magnificent
marble vases,
the War Vase,
by Coysevox,
illustrating the
crossing of the Rhine
(1672), and the
Peace Vase, carved
by Tubi.

*The Water
Parterre* 99

Nymph by Le Hongre
The Rhône by Tubi

The Loiret
by Regnaudin

"Then one should go straight to the top of the Latona slope and stop to take in the view of Latona, the lizards, the slopes, statues, the royal avenue, Apollo, the canal and then turn around to see the parterres and the Château". Louis XIV.

The entrances to the gardens in use today lead to the North and South Parterres. By going along the lateral façades of the central building, one comes to the Water Parterre.

In 1683, Jules Hardouin-Mansart and Le Nôtre decided to alter the parterre completely. Excavation work was carried out rapidly and, in 1685, visitors to the Park were able to admire the two magnificent lakes surrounded by their marble rims. A decorative ensemble of bronze figures was also planned but it was only partly carried out. These are the figures we see today. Between 1687 and 1690, the Keller brothers, metal-founders, cast in bronze in the Paris Arsenal the wax models brought to them by the sculptors in charge of the commissions.

Each fountain is adorned with four recumbent statues representing the Rivers of France, four groups of nymphs and four groups of children standing at each corner of the pool. Except for the latter, each groups bears the name of its sculptor and the date on which it was cast.

Around the north pool are the Marne and Seine, by Le Hongre and the Garonne and Dordogne, by Coysevox. The Seine, with its slow, regular current, is a taciturn old man crowned with vine-branches and reculs. The Marne, a young woman with a rather severe grace, holds a cornucopia. The Garonne, with its smiling face, holds a rudder while the Dordogne is surrounded by fruit, ears of corn and vines, and holds two overflowing urns under her arms.

Around the south pool are the Loire and Loiret, by Regnaudin and the Saône and Rhône, by Tuby. The Loire, the longest river in France flows through fertile land. It is crowned with reeds and lies amidst fruit and vegetables. The twin sources gushing forth at its sides symbolize the parallel courses of the Loire and the Allier. The Rhône, an impetuous river, has a severe face and a vigorous body. Its source bursts forth instead of flowing gently.

The Saône, crowned with flowers and vines, rests on ears of corn ; a little cupid at its sides presses grapes. This is the personification of "happy Burgundy".

The Water Parterre in summer

The Loire by Regnaudin

*The Water Parterre
in Winter*

*The Hours: "Daybreak"
by G. Marsy*

2 - THE FOUNTAINS OF THE ANIMALS

One cannot separate from the unique ensemble of the Water Parterre the two Fountains of the Animals, completed in three years, from 1684 to 1687. They flank the stairway leading to the Fountain of Latona.

The water from these square, raised pools, surrounded on three sides by the fences of the groves, falls into two smaller ones lower down, on the same level as the Water Parterre. On the upper rim, groups of animals cast in bronze by the Keller brothers confront each other.

Three statues stand around each of these pools.

This Fountain of the Animals is also called the "Fountain of Daybreak" after the nearby statue by Gaspard Marsy which lies to the south. In the foreground are the statues of Flora, by Magnier, and Water, by Le Gros.

The statues of fighting animals on the rim represent a tiger killing a bear and a bloodhound bringing down a stag, carved after models by Houzeau.

To the north, opposite the "Fountain of Daybreak", stands the second Fountain of the Animals, called the "Fountain of Diana" in honour of the statue by

The Elements:
"Air" by Le Hongre

The Hours: "Diana"
by Desjardins

Desjardins close by. It symbolizes "Evening" and frames the fountain with Venus or "Noon", by Gaspard Marsy.

Opposite the "Fountain of Daybreak", on the other side of Diana, is one of the finest pieces of 17th century garden sculpture: a young woman holding down her veils blown about by the wind; she symbolizes Air and is the work of Le Hongre.

On the upper rim, the two fighting lions, one with a boar, the other with a wolf, are by Van Clève and Raon.

The quality of the decoration of these Fountains is quite remarkable.

The four groups of animals are an impressive example of 17th century animal sculpture and the six statues, which were part of the 1674 commission, are among the finest in the gardens.

From the Fountain of the Animals, the visitor may admire at sufficient distance the magnificent façade of the château, over 1360 feet long, which is reflected in the two large pools of the Water Parterre.

From the same observation-point, he may look in the opposite direction beyond the Parterre of Latona towards the Royal Avenue which continues the Grand Canal as far as the horizon.

*Fountain
of Diana*

3 - THE PARTERRE OF LATONA

A great staircase of three flights and two gentle slopes adorned with vases and statues lead from the Water Parterre to the Parterre of Latona.

The latter consists of three fountains: the Fountain of Latona and the two Lizard Fountains.

The main fountain, which existed at the time of Louis XIII, was adorned as early as 1670 with a group representing Latona, with her two children, Diana and Apollo at her feet, imploring Jupiter to avenge her against the peasants of Lycia who scorned her and were turned into frogs by the ruler of Olympus. The group formerly stood on a rock in the centre of the pool and it was then surrounded by six frogs half-emerging from the water, while 24 others were placed on the lawn around the pool.

The design of the Fountain was altered as early as 1689, probably after designs by Jules Hardouin-Mansart. It is now composed of three concentric marble bases on top of which the statue of Latona, raised on a stand, now looks towards the Grand Canal. Each tier contains carvings of frogs, turtles and men and women with frogs' legs and

Sun
Vase

Latona and her children
Apollo and Diana

The Fountain of Latona
and east-west view

Marble vases
from the Parterre of Latona

heads, from which water gushes forth in more than 50 jets. The Latona group is of white marble, while the animals are of lead and were once gilded.

The Lizard Fountains, placed symmetrically in the centres of the two parterres of flower and lawn in the Horseshoe, also illustrate the legend of the metamorphosis of the Lycian peasants. They were carved in lead by the Marsy brothers. The parterres are lined with marble vases, the work of Dugoulon, Drouilly, Cornu, Hardy, etc., and some are copies of classical models.

Along the slopes stand statues which, apart from the three carved after Le Brun's sketches (on the left, Epic Poetry, by Tubi, Fire, by Dossier and, on the right, Melancholy, by La Perdrix), were copied from classical originals by students of the Academy of France in Rome, founded in 1670.

At the western end of the right slope once stood the Nymph with a Shell, by Coysevox (Louvre Museum), replaced by a modern replica. Opposite is a copy by Magnier of the famous classical statue of the Dying Gladiator.

The Half-Moon, in front of the Green Carpet, is decorated with terms by Houzeau, Dedieu, Van Clèves, Le Gros, and 4 groups carved after classical statues.

The Lizard
Fountain

4 - THE SOUTH PARTERRE

The South Parterre is reached by a central staircase framed by two of the oldest pieces of sculpture in the Park: the Children with Sphinxes. The bronze Cupids were designed in 1660 by Sarrazin, cast by Duval and placed on the marble sphinx carved by Lerambert. At the northern extremity of the balustrade separating the parterre from the groves stands the fine replica of a classical statue by Van Clève of Ariadne Sleeping. The only ornamentation of the South Parterre, adorned by two very simple circular pools, is its incomparable floral décor, which earned it the name of the Parterre of Flowers.

*The Children
with Sphinxes*

*Bronze Vase
of the South Parterre*

"One should then turn left and pass between the Sphinxes; one should pause for a moment before the fountain to observe the sheaf and the expanse of water; on arriving at the Sphinxes, one should stop to behold the south parterre..."
Louis XIV.

Besides the central stairway, four staircases between the two sphinxes leading to the South Parterre are flanked by marble vases. On the copings to the north, east and west, which line the terraces overlooking this parterre on three sides, stand bronze vases.

*The South
Parterre*

From June to October, the richest colours meet the visitor's gaze in the flowerbeds designed by Le Nôtre and the bronze vases carved by Ballin.

"After that, one goes straight to the top of the Orangery from where one will see the parterre of orange-trees and the Lake of the Swiss Guards. One turns right, one goes up between the bronze Apollo and the Lantin and pauses at the front section from where one sees Bacchus and Saturn". Louis XIV.

5 - THE ORANGERY

This colossal building, constructed by Jules Hardouin-Mansart from 1684 to 1686 below the South Parterre, replaced Le Vau's Orangery, which was considered too small. It consists of a central gallery, 504 feet long, extended by two lateral ones beneath the Stairways of the Hundred Steps. These two galleries are lit by twelve large arched windows. In front of the main gallery lies the beautiful Orangery parterre, consisting of six lawns and a round pool. During the reign of Louis XIV, the Orangery sheltered 2,000 orange-trees and 1,000 oleanders, pomegranates and rare trees. These were taken outside during the warm season and placed along the pathways of the parterre. This tradition is still respected in our time. The Orangery Parterre is closed off to the south by a balustrade overlooking a ditch and, to the east and west, by railings at the bottom of the Stairways of the Hundred Steps. The pillars of these gateways support four groups of sculpture: Zephyr

The south front
of the huge Orangery

"One descends the right slope of the Orangery and enters the garden of orange-trees, one then goes straight to the fountain from where one will contemplate the Orangery, one walks along the paths of tall orange-trees, then into the covered Orangery, and one leaves by the vestibule on the Labyrinth side". Louis XIV.

*The Orangery Parterre
and Lake of the Swiss Guards* 115

and Flora, and Venus and Adonis, by Le Conte, to the west on the garden side, and Aurora and Cephalus, and Vertumnus and Pomona, by Le Gros, to the east. Beyond the Orangery Parterre, on the other side of the road that leads to St-Cyr, lies the splendid Lake of the Swiss Guards, (dug on the site of a pool and marsh). As it had been planned in 1665, it was octagonal and smaller in size. From 1678 onwards, new excavation work was carried out by the Regiment of the Swiss Guards who left their name to the lake. The rounded ends were added in 1682 making the lake 2,237 feet long and 78 feet wide. As on the Grand Canal, nautical festivities often took place there under the *Ancien Régime*. Some of the dug out soil was used in the making of the Mall, which extended along the whole west length of the lake. Pall-mall was a very fashionable game during the reign of Louis XIV. At the extremity of the lake, which ends in the shape of a farthingale at the foot of the Satory hill, was placed the equestrian statue of Louis XIV by Bernini, which had been transformed into Marcus Curtius in 1685 by Girardon. This Italian work, which did not please the King, decorated several places in the Park before finally being exiled there in 1688.

Versailles seen from Satory by J.-B. Martin (1690)

6 - THE QUEEN'S GROVE

The Queen's Grove as we see it today was created in 1774-1775 during the replantation of the Park ordered by Louis XVI. It is a garden in the English style and replaces the famous labyrinth of Versailles which was built in 1673 after plans by Le Nôtre.

In each bend of a multitude of little alleys a fountain was tucked away (39 in all).

The subject of each of them had been taken from Aesop's fables and summed up in a quatrain by Benserade engraved in the stand. The lead animals were painted from nature. The ponds themselves were decorated with rockwork.

At the entrance of the Labyrinth two statues of Aesop and Cupid welcomed visitors. These works, of a rare naturalistic quality, were carved by the best sculptors of Louis XIV's reign: Le Hongre, Mazeline, Houzeau, Tubi etc...

This charming part of Versailles, which received so much praise in every 17th century guide-book unfortunately deteriorated to such an extent that disappeared in 1774.

A few sculptures that it used to belong to this splendid ensemble still exist and are kept in the Palace of Versailles.

7 - THE ROCKWORK GROVE
OR THE BALLROOM

This grove, created from 1681 to 1683, used to be called the Ballroom "because of the sort of arena on which one dances when it pleases his Majesty to hold a celebration". The "arena", a round marble platform, disappeared at the beginning of the 18th century, but the surrounding rising tiers and rockwork are still there to make the grove famous. The water streams down in a cascade on the rockwork, which is made of Madagascan shells.

The orchestra used to sit at the top. The carved gilt-lead vases of the topmost tier are by Le Comte and Le Hongre, while the candle-stands at the bottom were made by Le Gros, Mazeline, Massou and Jouvenet. On either side of the entrances, banks support the tiers where the spectators used to sit during the festivities which were very numerous at the end of the 17th century according to the diary kept by the Marquess of Dangeau. The bas-reliefs on the vases represent "nymphs dancing, children revelling, Neptune and Amphitrite and children mounted on dolphins, "while the candlestands are decorated with masks, trophies, musical instruments and dancing nymphs and bacchantes".

Gilded vase
from the Rockwork Grove

"One enters the Labyrinth and, after going as far as the ducks and the dog, one returns to leave by the exit near Bacchus. One then visits the Ballroom, going right around it, and into the centre, and one leaves by the end of the Latona slope". Louis XIV. *The gilded candlestands and vases of the Rockwork Grove enable us to imagine more fully the rich décor of the Park of yesteryear, when the gilded ornamentation of the pools and groves glittered on the cask of dark water and foliage.*

"From the end of the Latona slope one goes straight to the observation point, looking, in passing, at the small satyr fountain in one of the groves; on arriving at the observation point, one should pause to gaze at the slopes, vases, statues, Lizards, Latona and the château; on the other side, the royal avenue, Apollo, the canal, the bouquets of groves, Flora, Saturn, to the right, Ceres, to the left, Bacchus". Louis XIV.

The Parterre of Latona

8 - THE OBSERVATION POINT

The two slopes flanking the Parterre of Latona lead to a half-moon at which the Green Carpet ends.

This half-moon is called the "Observation Point". It was there that Louis XIV wished visitors to stop in order to admire the various views of the gardens: beyond the Parterre of Latona facing the château and, in the other direction, the Grand Canal, which extends the east-west axis as far as the horizon, while, to the north and south, wide shady avenues lead one's gaze towards the Fountains of Ceres to the north and to that of Bacchus to the south.

Four marble groups, including Tubi's Laocoön, adorn the entrance to the Green Carpet.

Behind the curtain of trees, one catches a glimpse of the Quincunxes which have replaced the former groves: to the north, the Dauphin's Grove and to the south the Candelabra Grove.

These are glades with a simple lawn in their centre, surrounded by regularly spaced trees. Each of the Quincunxes is decorated by eight terms executed in Rome after Poussin's models for the château of Vaux-le-Vicomte.

Entrance to the Green Carpet
Tubi's Laocoön

9 - AUTUMN AND WINTER
THE FOUNTAINS OF THE SEASONS

The four Fountains of the Seasons are situated at the four crossroads formed by the main avenues of the park. North of the Green Carpet are the Fountains of Flora and Ceres, to the south those of Saturn and Bacchus.

These four fountains were executed after sketches by Le Brun from 1672 onwards.

The Fountains of Bacchus or Autumn (1673-1675) is octagonal in shape. The Marsy brothers have represented the god crowned with vine-branches. He is surrounded by little satyrs reclining on an abundant harvest, its bunches of grapes dipping into the water. "This is the island of Autumn... the god of wine lies on the golden harvest. What secret has his drunkenness revealed to him for him that he should smile so mysteriously... His figure has the robustness of the bodies of young wild animals and the grace of feminine beauty. He throws handfuls of grapes into the urn while, around him, goat-footed children drink from vessels or press the vermilion fruit between their lips.

Here, a satiated little satyr has fallen asleep, there another attempts to make a goat swallow the contents of a ewer"...

The Fountains of Saturn or Winter (1675-1677) is circular. The god Saturn, aging and sad, lies on a rock covered with icicles, seaweed and shells. "He has the great outspread wings of Time and... the deep wrinkles of the years, on his lips the bitter expression of the gods who must live forever and would prefer to die".

He is surrounded by young children "one of whom fans an imaginary fire with bellows. They call joyously to Spring from this cold snow of Winter". The group is the work of Girardon.

*Fountain
of Autumn*

"One descends towards Saturn and sees the candelabra in passing, one then turns back and goes to the royal island. One takes the path lined with sprays of water on either side; one visits the whole of the large pool, and, while at the end, one should stop to cast one's eyes over the bouquets, shells, pools, statues and porches. One then continues to the small pathway leading to Apollo and one enters at the end of the gallery; one goes right through it and leaves by the avenue leading to the Colonnade". Louis XIV.

10 - THE KING'S GARDEN

In 1817, the King's Garden replaced the Royal Island which was composed of two great pools: the Mirror or Farthingale (1672) and the Great Lake (1674-1683) separated by a path still. The Great Lake soon became a swamp covered with rushes and Louis XVIII had replaced an English garden with carefully tended shrubs created in front of the Mirror Pool.

The Hall of Classical Statues by J.-B. Martin

The Hall of Classical Statues or Water Gallery. Painting by J.-B. Martin, 1688. Through this oval grove once ran a central pathway lined with orange-trees, pruned yew-trees, pools and fountains. This pathway was surrounded by statues. Entirely rearranged in 1704, this grove became the Hall of Chestnut-Trees in the 18th century. It was adorned with classical busts and a statue. A small circular pool at each end is a reminder of its original decoration.

125

"One enters the Colonnade, goes into the centre and around it to take in the columns, arches, bas-reliefs, vases and pools. As one leaves, one should stop to look at the group by Guidy and then walk towards the royal avenue. One goes down it to Apollo where one should pause to contemplate the figures and vases of the royal avenue, Latona and the château; one will also see the canal. If, on the same day, one can visit the Menagerie and Trianon, one walks straight ahead to see the remaining fountains".
Louis XIV.

126

11 - THE COLONNADE

The Colonnade was built from 1685 onwards. This grove, with its striking architectural design, is the result of the close collaboration of Le Nôtre and Jules Hardouin-Mansart.

This perfectly circular peristyle measures 106 feet in diameter. 32 columns of the Ionic order made of violet brecciated, Languedoc or slate-blue marble, coupled with 32 Languedoc marble pilasters support arches and a white marble cornice bearing 32 urns. The triangular tympani between the arches are decorated with bas-reliefs most of which represent cupids playing music, thus evoking the original purpose of this grove, in which so many concerts took place.

The key-stones of the arches are adorned with heads of nymphs, naiads, etc. These various sculptures the work of Coysevox, Tubi, Le Hongre, Le Conte, Mazière and Granier.

Under each arch, wide basins of white marble form as many fountains. A circular white marble stairway in the centre of the Colonnade eads to the famous group executed in 1699 by Girardon, which represents the Rape of Persephone by Pluto. This work has been removed to protect it from bad weather.

The Colonnade Grove

12 - THE GREEN CARPET
AND THE FONTAIN OF APOLLO

The Green Carpet, or Royal Avenue, 1099 feet long and 210 feet wide, leads to the Fountain of Latona, that of Apollo and, beyond, to the Grand Canal. The central section of this avenue is formed by a wide lawn, after which the avenue was named. It is decorated with twelve marble statues and vases, most of which were carved during the 17th century by students of the Academy of France in Rome.

The Green Carpet leads to a half-moon adorned with twelve terms and statues. It was on this site, called *"Le Rondeau"*, that Sublet de Noyers, Louis XIII's Master of Buildings, had a pond dug as early as 1639.

Louis XIV had it altered and it was then given the name of the Pond of the Swans until 1671. At that time, the pool was again transformed and it received Tubi's splendid lead ensemble representing Apollo on his chariot drawn by four horses and surrounded by dolphins and tritons.

The quadrilobate pool is one of the largest in the park, 384 feet long and 285 feet wide.

Beyond this pool lies the Grand Canal, 5,118 feet long and 394 feet wide. It is intersected at its centre by an arm, 3,376 feet long, leading from the Menagerie to the Grand Trianon.

Digging was begun in 1667-1668, and it was practically completed by 1680. A great many festivities were held on this magnificent expanse of water where, as early as 1669, a whole flotilla of magnificently bedecked shallops and galliots would take the Court for boat rides. In 1679, the first gondola for the Canal was presented to Louis XIV by the Republic of Venice. In 1687, several Venetian gondoliers were placed in charge of the fleet and lived in the still existing buildings called Little Venice, situated at the end of the Canal.

The Royal Avenue
A sun flower vase

Pierre de Nolhac described Apollo's Chariot in the following terms: ''Morning has come; Apollo leaves the marine grotto with his wife, Tethys, after having rested. He is seen rising out of the waters in his shining chariot, casting rays of light before him... This powerful group is reflected in the changing mirror whose surface takes on all the hues of the sky while, round about, the mass of trees spreads its atmosphere of calm mystery... At dusk, the god's journey ends; in the pools on various levels, the colours of the sky fade away; silence grows with the shadows''.

13 - THE ENCELADUS

The Fountain of Enceladus was cast in lead by Marsy in 1676 and was formerly gilded. The subject is taken from the story of the fall of the Titans, who were crushed under the rocks of Mount Olympus after they had tried to scale it in spite of Jupiter.

The sculptor has represented the giant half-crushed beneath the rocks, trying to fight against death.

Aristaeus and Proteus by Slodtz (1723)

14 - THE GROVE OF THE DOMES

At the time of its creation in 1675, the centre of the pool contained a gilt-lead figure of Fame on a globe, sending forth a powerful jet of water from her trumpet.

From 1677 to 1678, Hardouin-Mansart built two white marble pavilions standing opposite each other, decorated with trophies and gilt-bronze bas-reliefs. Bet-

"One takes the little pathway leading to Flora, one goes to the baths of Apollo and walks around them to run one's eyes over the statues,

The Fountain of Enceladus

fountains and bas-reliefs. One passes by Enceladus, where one walks around only half the fountain and, after having looked at it, one leaves at the other end". Louis XIV.

ween these two pavilions were placed sculptures from the Grotto of Tethys: the famous groups of Apollo and his horses and the statues of Acis and Galatea. In the centre of the grove was an octagonal pool surrounded by a marble balustrade with gilt-bronze railings. A base adorned with 44 bas-reliefs representing the arms used by the various nations of the world enclosed the outside of the pool.

This grove fell into disrepair due to neglect. During the reign of Louis-Philippe, the statues, (which have been returned here today), were removed. Only the foundations of the pavilions remain, but the pool still has its magnificent bas-reliefs. The statues are of Galatea, by Tubi, Aurora, by Magnier, Acis, by Tubi, Daybreak, by Le Gros, Ino, by Rayol, a nymph, by Flamen and Arion, by Raon.

The Grove of the Domes

Arion by Raon

"One enters
the Council
Chamber,
goes as far as
Flora and
then turns back".
Louis XIV.

At the end of
an avenue which
leads away from
the Fountain of
Flora one catches
a glimpse of
the Obelisk Fountain
which "occupies
a vast area
divided up
geometric-
ally... until 1704,
the Grove of the
Banquet Hall or
Council Chamber
could be seen there.
This grove was
destroyed at the
same time as
the Mountain of
Water. This
large raised
pool was then
installed in its
place... with a
clump of
reeds in lead
in the centre
as its only
decorative element.

132 *Fountain
of Spring*

15 - SPRING AND SUMMER
THE FOUNTAINS
OF THE SEASONS

The Fountain of Flora or Spring (1672-1675) is also round and was carved by Tubi. The goddess, half-naked, rests on a bed of varied flowers, surrounded by young cupids playing at weaving garlands which "intertwine and tumble down to the water of the pool... Tubi has imagined her almost naked... the wife of Zephyr; her hand rests on a basket brimming over with cornflowers, anemones, all the flowers of the old gardens of France".

The Fountain of Ceres or Summer (1672-1674) is octagonal. This group, by Regnaudin, represents the goddess with a sickle in her hand, her head crowned with ears of corn. Around her, on the ground strewn with corn, lie naked cupids. "This work is not complete... until the spray falls in a sheaf... on to scattered harvest mingled with flowers of the fields. Ceres lies bending backwards amidst her gifts, looking blissfully at the liquid column which rises towards the foliage" and flows over the three cupids playing at her sides.

Modern restoration processes remind one that the lead groups decorating the Fountains of the Seasons were originally gilded.

Fountain of Summer

16 - FOUR GROVES AT THE NORTHERN END OF THE GARDENS

In the northern section of the gardens, Le Nôtre had created several groves which Louis XIV's itinerary invites us to enter. Only their sites remain today.

The Star Grove, in the centre of which stood quite a large fountain called the Mountain of Water, disappeared in 1704. Avenues radiating out from it evoke its former design.

The Grove of the Water Theatre situated further to the east was renowned for its hydraulic effects. Destroyed in the middle of the 18th century, it was replaced by a simple grassy bowl which was called the Green Ring.

On either side of the Water Avenue were two large groves. On the right, the Grove of the Three Fountains consisted of a series of cascades and pools making use of the declivity of the ground for their effect. On the left, the Grove of the Triumphal Arch, executed by Le Nôtre from 1677 to 1683, was also decorated by three fountains and an "arch entirely of gilded wrought-iron", erected to the glory of Louis XIV. This grove was destroyed in 1775. All that remains of it today is the groups of France in Triumph, the work of Tubi and Coysevox.

The Water Theatre Grove
gouache by Jean Cotelle

Grove of the Three Fountains
painting by Jean Cotelle

"One goes around the Dragon and beholds the sprays and pool of Neptune. One then goes to the Triumphal arch where one should notice the diversity of the fountains, sprays, expanse of water, the bowls, statues and various water effects. One leaves by the Dragon, takes the Children's Avenue and, on arriving at the stone which lies between the two lower ponds, one should turn around to cast one's eyes on all the sprays of Neptune and the Dragon; one then continues to walk up this avenue". Louis XIV.

*The Sun Horses groomed by Tritons
by Guérin*

17 - THE BATHS OF APOLLO

The Grove of Apollo's Bath, as we see it nowadays, dates from 1775, the time of the replantation of the Versailles Park.

It replaced a famous grove which had been created during the reign of Louis XIV, from 1670 to 1676, and was called The Marsh. On this site Jules Hardouin-Mansart prepared a new grove destined to receive the groups of the Sun Horses, which had been in the grove of the Domes since the destruction of the famous Grotto of Tethys.

This ensemble, which was carved between 1672 and 1677, is composed of three groups: the central one represents Apollo being tended by the Nymphs, with four main statues by Girardon and the other three, further back, by Renaudin.

The two groups of the Sun Horses being groomed by Tritons are by Marsy — group with the rearing horse — and by Gilles de Guérin — group with the horse drinking. The three groups were sheltered from the rain under gilt lead canopies designed by Mansart.

In front of the three fountains, standing on a base, were a small semi-circular pond and a stretch of sand.

This state lasted until 1778. In 1776, two years after Louis XVI's order to replant the Park, the painter Hubert-Robert was asked to rearrange the Baths of Apollo. The project was carried out from 1778 to 1781.

Hubert-Robert's grove is in the then popular style of the Anglo-Chinese garden. A huge artificial rock adorned with columns was built; it is supposed to represent the Palace of Tethys.

The main group, by Girardon and Regnaudin, is situated in the central grotto, while the groups by marsy and Guérin stand on platforms lower down. A cascade and a shady glade complete this ensemble.

Apollo tended by Nymphs
by Girardon and Regnaudin 137

To the north of the gardens, between, the Star Grove and the Green Ring, and far from the avenues with their visitors to the gardens, a circular pool with a rock in the centre is concealed from view. This is the Children's Island, a masterpiece of spontaneity by Hardy (1710). On the rock, six naked children play with fowers while two others splash about in the water. The charming grace of their poses will not fail to delight the wanderer who discovers this isolated grove.

The Fountain of the Children's Island

18 - THE DRAGON FOUNTAIN AND THE FOUNTAIN OF NEPTUNE

These two fountains constitute at the North end of the Park an ensemble which was executed during the reigns of Louis XIV and Louis XV, that is to say over almost a century. It was from 1679 onwards that the pool called "Out of the Dragon", better known today as the Fountain of Neptune, was created. Le Nôtre had planned the semicircular shape of the Fountain of Neptune as early as 1678. It was executed from 1679 to 1684 under the direction of Le Nôtre, and then of Jules Hardouin-Mansart, in collaboration with Le Brun for the decoration. Three stone tiers in the shape of an amphitheatre constitute the semicircular part. The diameter is composed of a retaining-wall of irregular shape edged with a gutter. The Fountain was begun during the reign of Louis XIV but completed only in the middle of Louis XV's reign in 1741.

Formerly on the gutter were eight lead groups of children bearing bronze basins which, in 1688, were used to decorate the half-moon around the Dragon Fountain and the end of the Avenue of the Marmosets.

In 1684, a new decoration was created: bowls and shells ornamented the retaining wall, the top of which then held twenty-two gilt-lead vases. Against the wall and in the centre was placed the group of Neptune and Amphitrite by Houzeau and Raon. Six other carved groups, which were probably not executed, were planned to accompany it.

Twenty-two fountains in the gutter, twenty-two coming out of the vases and six sprays gushing out of the front section of the pool played before the King for the first time on 17th of May, 1685.

The financial difficulties at the end of the reign prevented the completion of work on this magnificent hydraulic ensemble, which from then on, for want of regular maintenance, fell into disrepair. The architect Gabriel had to rebuild it almost entirely from 1733 to 1734. In particular he straightened the retaining-wall and somewhat modified the dimen-

Fountain of Neptune
Sea-Dragon ridden by a Cupid 139

sions. After this restoration work, the Directory of Buildings organised a competition for the decoration of the pool. The prize was won by Lambert Sigisbert Adam. He was the sculptor who carved the central group of Neptune and Amphitrite. The god and goddess are sitting in a large conch in the rococo style, surrounded and supported by sea-animals. This vigorous, boisterous work is signed and dated 1740. On its left, in 1739, Bouchardon also modelled the lead figure of Proteus sitting on a sea-unicorn. On the right of the central group the god Ocean, reclining on a conch supported by fishes, is the work of J.-B. Lemoine (1740). At the extremity of the pool are two giant dragons ridden by two cupids, the work of Bouchardon. This pool, as we see it today, was inaugurated on 14th August 1741 by Louis XV, who could then admire the ninety-nine magnificent water-effects for which this ensemble became famous from then on.

The perimeter of this pool is adorned with two statues of Berenice and Faustina, on either side of the important group "The King's Fame" carried out in Rome in 1686 by the Italian sculptor, Domenico Guidi.

The circular-shaped Pool of the Dragon—133 feet in diameter—is adorned with several lead groups scattered on the waters: they are modern copies which, in 1889, took the place of the entirely ruined 17th century works. They stand around the large lead Dragon, formerly gilded, the work of Gaspard Marsy.

Four dolphins swim around the monster, which little cupids ridings swans ara about to fight with their arrows.

The particularity of this work was that, under the reign of Louis XIV, it could throw water to two different heights, depending on whether the King was present or not (36 feet and 90 feet). The greater height (90 feet) is that of the present water-display.

The Dragon
Fountain

The Fountain of Neptune
painted by J.-B. Martin

"One goes to the mountain by turning into the little avenue ich runs off before entering the centre of the Star and, on arriving there, one walks around the mountain. Then one passes by Ceres before going to the heatre. There, one will notice the changes made and one should contemplate the jets of water in the arcades. One leaves by the end of the North parterre slope and enters the Marsh; one walks around it. ne enters the three fountains at the upper end, escends and, after having seen the fountains on the three levels, one leaves by the avenue leading to the Dragon". Louis XIV.

24 - THE WATER AVENUE

The shady walk leading from the Dragon Fountain to the North Parterre is called the *Water Avenue,* or, more appealingly, the Avenue of the Marmosets.

Its decoration was, it seems, imagined by the doctor and architect, Claude Perrault, in 1668. It is therefore part of the ensemble composed of the Pyramid Fountain and the Bathing Nymphs.

The first fourteen groups of children facing each other in pairs on either side of the alley were placed there in 1670. This first ensemble was completed in 1678 by a second one of eight groups, which were intended to ornament the half-moon at the end of the Water Avenue. In 1684, when the project of decorating the Water Parterre with bronze statues was created, it was decided to replace the twenty-two lead groups by similar works of bronze, which we see here today. The major theme is childhood, but it is expressed in a wide variety of figures since we meet in turn tritons, cupids, child musicians, little girls, young satyrs, little fishermen, and terms. In each group three figures stand in the centre of a round, white marble pond. They bear a pink Languedoc marble bowl from which the water cascades into the pond, surrounding the little bearers with a liquid veil. Many artists worked on this ensemble and their name will be familiar to the observant visitor to the Park.

Successively, we find:

1 - three tritons, by Le Gros; 2 - three little dancers, by Le Gros; 3 - two cupids and a little girl, by Le Hongre; 4 - three children leaning on a tree-trunk, by Lerambert; 5 - three child musicians by Lerambert; 6 - three little satyrs, by Le Gros; 7 - three terms, by Lerambert; 8 - two little girls and a little boy with fishes, by Mazeline; 9 - three little hunters, by Mazeline; 10 - three childreen, by Buirette; 11 - three little girls, by Buirette.

Entwined Tritons
of the Water Avenue

25 - THE BATHING NYMPHS

At the entrance to the Water Avenue lies the famous fountain of the Bathing Nymphs, created, in part, by the talented François Girardon. The decoration of the walls bordering the fountain on three sides consists of a series of bas-reliefs formerly of gilt lead which are separated by terms.

The bas-relief on the far wall, which gave its name to the fountain, is the work of Girardon. In his Memoirs, Charles Perrrault **attributes the design of the bas-relief to Claude Perrault, (the writer's brother) and adds that the sculptor Girardon executed** the figures "even more prettily than they appear in the drawing". It is also certain that this work was inspired by a painting by Domenichino. It represents a group of naked nymphs joyfully splashing about in a river lined with climbing plants and reeds. This bas-relief carved with great charm and gentleness was inspired by a painting by the Italian painter, Domenico Zampieri, called Domenichino. This lead sculpture is flanked by bas-reliefs representing streams and children carrying baskets of flowers.

On the lateral walls, bas-reliefs gradually decreasing in size represent nymphs and cupids borne by dolphins and fish. Like the

Pyramid Fountain, this one is decorated with a whole acquatic world, so successfully created by Le Hongre and Le Gros. Unfortunately, the fountain of the Bathing Nymphs faces north because of the declivity of the ground and therefore never receives the sun.

"Bathing Nymphs" lead bas-relief by Girardon (central motif) 143

The bas-relief by Girardon, one of the finest pieces of sculpture in the gardens, was described by Pierre de Nolhac as follows: "Eleven nymphs, modest in their nudity, splash about in the waters of a river. The dream landscape seems almost real by virtue of the colours of the lead which glisten from years of being polished by the water... This long sections is rounded off at each end by two nymphs seated in the foreground, holding the drapery which is to enfold them after their bath. The one on the right reclines on a rock... nearby, a naiad flees towards the trees... a third companion laughs at the drops of water flying about. In the background, two young girls bathing seem to withdraw from the others... (in the centre) are four beautiful girls taking part joyfully in a lively skirmish... a fifth naiad who has escaped from the fray, laughs heartily... she faces another nymph, stretched out beside her, who completes the composition, so full of movement. The curved lines skilfully create the most exquisite harmony; the bodies of the young girls are as supple as twining plants, they seem alive, one can see them playing, and hear them laughing in the faintly gilded air, in the water whose pink hues mingle gently with azure ones."

"Bathing Nymphs"

The Water Avenue

"*One should stop at the bottom of the Nape and look at the bas-reliefs and the rest of this fountain. Then one goes on to the Pyramid where one should pause for a moment before going back up to the château by the marble staircase between the Knifegrinder and the Modest Venus; at the top of the staircase one should stop to survey the North parterre, the statues, vases, crowns, the Pyramid and what one can see of Neptune, and then one leaves the garden by the same gate by which one entered*". Louis XIV.

The Pyramid
Fountain

*Winter
by Girardon* 145

21 - THE NORTH PARTERRE

The itinerary we have followed to visit the gardens, and which corresponds roughly to that described by Louis XIV himself, takes us back to the château via the North Parterre.

This parterre consists of wide stretches of triangular lawns slightly raised and lined with a border of box-tree hedges. These hedges also form compartments for the flowers planted there in abundance.

As one comes from the Water Avenue, one sees, at the end of the central avenue of the North Parterre, the Pyramid Fountain by Girardon. Designed after a sketch by the painter Le Brun, it was begun in 1669 and completed in 1672. The Pyramid consists of four superimposed bowls of decreasing size. Four large double-tailed tritons swimming in the circular pool support the lowest bowl in which four young tritons hold up the second, narrower bowl. In the latter, four diving dolphins bear the third bowl on their upright tails. Finally, four crayfish are curved between this and the upper bowl surmounted with an urn from which the water gushes forth to cascade in great surges from one bowl to another.

On either side of the central avenue, towards the

lower section of the North Parterre, the hedges surround two circular pools called the Crown Fountains. The work of Le Hongre and Tubi, they consists of reclining sirens and tritons which once held up a crown with a *fleur-de-lis*. The Parterre is sheltered from cold winds by the tall trees lining it on the Water Avenue side as well as by the massive architecture of the North Wing. During the fine season,

Autumn by Regnaudin
The Crown Fountain

The Pyramid Fountain
America by Guérin

the form of a faun with a cunning smile, by Byster, and Pastoral Poetry, by Granier.

There are also three of the Four Humours, Phlegm, by Lespagnandelle, and, on either side of the Bathing Nymphs, Choler, by Houzeau, standing opposite Sanguinity, by Jouvenet. Three of the Four Seasons form part of these statues: Ceres, by Hutinot, symbolizing Summer, Bacchus, by Regnaudin, representing Autumn, and "a melancholy old man carved by Girardon", symbolizing Winter.

The Four Parts of the World are symbolized by statues of women.

Asia, by Roger, holds a perfume vase, America, by Guerin, carries a quiver and a crown of feathers, Africa, by Cornu, wears an elephant's head and Europa, by Mazeline wears a helmet and holds a shield.

One of the Four Elements, Earth, by Massou, with a lion at its feet, stands near Night, by Raon, with her robes edged with stars and holding a torch. Several vases and five terms representing orators complete this ensemble of marble statues in the North Parterre.

Finally, at the top of the central staircase leading to the château, two bronze statues crouch on either side of the steps.

the compartments of box-tree are filled with a profusion of flowers of the most varied and lively colours.

Statues stand along the avenues which run along the parterre to the north and west.

Most were part of the 1674 commission and were placed where we now see them as early as 1686.

Among them are the Four Types of Poetry: Epic Poetry, by Drouilly, at the foot of the château, crowned with the laurel leaves of glory, Satirical Poetry, in

The North

They are copies of classical models: the Knifegrinder, by Foggini and the Modest Venus, by Coysevox, of which the original is in the Louvre.

On the marble coping which lines the terrace overlooking the South Parterre stand bronze vases with various types of ornamentation cast by Ambroise Duval after models by Claude Ballin; two of the vases are by Michel Anguier.

The central section of the château seen from the North Parterre

The Hours: "Night" by Raon

TRIANON

The building of stone and marble we see here today is not the first château built at Trianon.

In 1670, the architect Le Vau built the so-called Porcelain Trianon, its exterior decorated with blue and white china tiles, on the site of a village bought by Louis XIV in 1668. This first Trianon was a fragile building used for taking light refreshments. In 1687, it was already on the point of falling into ruin. Moreover, its small size and its style no longer suited the King.

Jules Hardouin-Mansart was commissioned to build the Marble Trianon now here. The idea of the peristyle linking the two wings running into the gardens came from Robert de Cotte. A gallery was added at right angles to the right wing and, perpendicular to this gallery, the Trianon-in-the-Woods wing. The doors and windows overlooking both the courtyard and gardens are rythmed with pink Languedoc marble pilasters.

Louis XV had Jussieu and Richard create a botanical garden to the east of the Grand Trianon. In 1750, he had Gabriel construct a small pavilion there (the French Pavilion) and, from 1749 to 1753, a menagerie. Soon afterwards, the sovereign wanted a small château erected there: the Small Trianon, built from 1762 to 1768.

After his grandfather's death in 1774, Louis XVI gave the estate of the Small Trianon to Queen Marie-Antoinette as a gift. She ordered Hubert-Robert to replace Louis XV's botanical gardens by a pleasure park. With the collaboration of the architect Mique, Hubert-Robert created successively the Temple of Love, the Belvedere (1778), the Theatre (1780)

and finally, the Hamlet, of which ten of the twelve cottages are still standing (1783). The Small Trianon was turned into a café during the Revolution and restored and refurnished for the first time by Napoleon at the same time as the Grand Trianon.

While the furnishings in the Grand Trianon today conjure up the pomp of the Empire, the Small Trianon has been dedicated to the memory of Marie-Antoinette ever since Empress Eugénie decided, in 1867, to organize an exhibition to honour this Queen. Restored by order of General de Gaulle, President of the Republic, the Grand Trianon is now used for official receptions.

The Main Gateway
of the Grand Trianon

The Peristyle
seen from the Upper Garden 151

VISITE DU GRAND TRIANON

18 — Wing of Trianon in the Woods

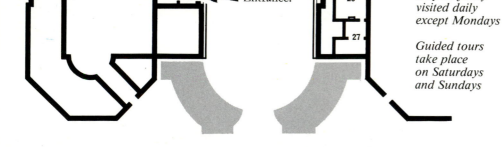

May be freely visited daily except Mondays

Guided tours take place on Saturdays and Sundays

Entrance.

THE GRAND TRIANON

THE ENTRANCE ROOMS

Before reaching the Mirror Drawing-Room, the visitors must go through four drawing-rooms newly created for receptions. The first objet d'art to greet the visitor in the entrance drawing-room is a bust of Napoleon I (by Bosio), as a reminder that it was the Emperor who ordered the refurnishing of the Grand Trianon. In the next drawing-room, a large painting by Allegrain depicts the "Northern Parterre".
The third drawing-room is furnished with seats from the châ-

teau of Saint-Cloud as well as a gilt-bronze pedestal table.
The wood panelling in this drawing-room is hung with a set of paintings depicting the groves in the Versailles gardens. In a gallery with its curtains restored like all those on the windows at Trianon, are hung engravings dedicated to the campaigns of Louis XIV. This gallery leads to the Boudoir

The Boudoir

A Lampstand of the Mirror Drawing Room

giving access both to the historical apartments (on the right) and those decorated by the National Furniture Foundation for the foreign Heads of State and their attendants (on the left, no admittance). Furniture by Jacob is exhibited there and special notice should be taken of the "arch-of-triumph" desk commissioned by Josephine.

6 - THE MIRROR DRAWING ROOM

This room is undoubtedly one of the most interesting and original in Trianon because of its decoration of mirrors and its cornice adorned with children, symbolizing War and Peace.

It reminds us of Louis XIV's Council Chamber at Versailles after it had been enlarged and entirely transformed under Louis XV. Its particularly pleasant situation has always made the Mirror Drawing-Room one of the most important rooms of Trianon.

Louis XIV's Council Chamber until 1703, then the Cabinet of the Grand Dauphin, this room was again a Council Chamber under Louis XVI and finally under Louis-Philippe.

For a while, this room was the Cabinet of the Empress Marie-

*The Mirror
Drawing Room*

The Empress's
Bedchamber

It was only recently that this room, which was formerly Louis XIV's then the Grand Dauphin's bedchamber, again received the proportions it had in 1700.

A partition had actually been built under Napoleon, hiding the two fine columns that now constitute an elegant separation in the middle of the room. This partition had been designed to create a drawing-room before the room itself, which always remained a bedroom.

The seats and the balustrade in the alcove, which were ordered from Marcion, and the dressing-table delivered by Baudouin date from the Empire. The rest of the furniture, which, for the most part, is anterior to the "July Monarchy", was placed there in 1837: visitors should notice particularly the bed, delivered for Napoleon at the Tuileries. Louis XVIII used it and died there. It was transported to Trianon under Louis-Philippe, who had his initials put at the head. The chest-of-drawers bought by Charles X in 1827 is the work of Werner and Deniere. It was also brought here in 1837. The two linen chests, which date from 1809,

Louise. This is the state to which the room has been partly restored and which explains the presence of a piano-forte and several small tables : a writing table, a drawing table, etc. The seats now decorating the room come from other drawing-rooms in the Grand Trianon.

The religious theme of the Antechamber, formerly the Chapel of the Grand Trianon, symbolized by the cornice sculpted in grapes and ears of corn, is also evidenced by two paintings representing Saint Luke and Saint Mark. The Saint John which can be seen in the photograph was transfered to the Chamber. The pictorial décor of the Courtiers' Drawing-Room includes two replicas from the studio of Jean-Baptiste Van Loo hung on the side walls : one represents Louis XV in a suit of armor, and the other, on the opposite wall, Maria Leczinska.

*The Chapel
Antechamber*

received Marie-Amélie's monogram in 1837.

8 - THE CHAPEL ANTECHAMBER

It is difficult to imagine in our day that this antechamber was the Chapel of the Grand Trianon from 1687 onwards. If we look at it more carefully, however, we shall notice the frieze, where ears of corn and grapes are mingled, their union symbolizing Holy Communion under the two species.
The altar was placed in an alcove which was closed by two doors facing the windows. The alcove is still to be seen nowadays. First used as a dining-room by Madame Mère, the room was later turned into a Drawing Room by the Empress Marie-Louise as well as by Queen Marie-Amélie.
Of the Imperial furniture, there only remains a table by Martin decorated with the signs of the Zodiac. The seats were formerly at Saint-Cloud.

9 - THE COURTIERS' DRAWING ROOM

This antechamber is one of the first creations of the Marble Trianon. We should notice its vaulted ceiling and, on the cornice, its fine military trophy. The Courtiers' antechamber of Louis XIV's apartment, this room was still used as such at the time of the Grand Dauphin.

Under Napoleon it was first the antechamber of Napoleon's mother and then a dining-room for the attendants of the Emperor and Empress.

In 1836 it was the room of the ushers of King Louis-Philippe's wife, Queen Marie-Amélie.

Above the fireplace, the picture representing the Family of the Grand Dauphin is by Delutel after Mignard. It had been ordered by Monsieur, Louis XIV's brother, for his mansion at Saint-Cloud.

The painting represents the Grand Dauphin (1661-1711), son of Louis XIV, in the company of his wife, Maria-Anna of Bavaria (1660-1690). They had three children. The eldest of the three, the Duc de Bourgogne (1682-1712), who later became Louis XV's father, is shown standing to the right.

In the foreground, the Duc d'Anjou (1683-1746) sits on a cushion; proclaimed King of Spain in 1700, he took the name of Philip V. The Duc de Berry (1686-1714) is shown on his mother's knees.

The tour of the left wing ends with this room, that is, in reverse order from what one would logi-

cally expect. The normal entrances to the apartments in the left and right wings of the Grand Tria-

non were the two rooms at either end of the Peristyle with its marble floor. This antechamber,

like the Round Drawing Room further on, also has an elegant marble floor.

"The Family of the Grand Dauphin" 157

11 - THE ROUND DRAWING ROOM

After crossing the Peristyle, one enters the right wing by a circular room with a magnificent floor of marble.

This antechamber is undoubtedly one of the finest creations of the *"Grand Siècle"* at Trianon.

Originally, four similar niches opened into this room. Those on the windows side have been kept to this day while those facing them were closed by two *"tambour"*, doors designed by Gabriel.

The one on the right was intended for the altar of a chapel and that on the left to become a small antechamber for the King's apartments. The reason for this is that when Louis XV stayed frequently at Trianon after 1750 he wished to have a chapel nearer to his apartments than the one in the left wing.

During the whole of the 19th century, this Round Drawing Room was used as the Ushers' Room. Louis-Philippe had disfigured it by having the fireplace modified and the pavement replaced by a floor. It was returned to its former state during the latest restoration work on the residence.

One should notice the floral paintings by Desportes and the two large works by Verdier.

10 - THE PERISTYLE

The most original work of architecture in the Grand Trianon, the Peristyle has a twofold purpose: it was to link the courtyard and the gardens enhancing them by its fine columns and to connect the left and right wings by a loggia which recalls certain Italian constructions. It was used as a summer dining-room under Louis XIV. Disfigured by glass doors in 1810, the Peristyle was used as a large vestibule adorned with statues and vases under Louis-Philippe. Because of its dimensions it was chosen for Marshall Bazaine's trial in 1873. It was only in 1910 that it regained its former appearance.

The Left Wing
seen from the Peristyle

12 - THE MUSIC ROOM

The name of "Music Room" which is still often given to this room comes from the fact that it was used as such under Louis XIV.

In fact its purpose was triple until 1691: it was at the same time the first antechamber of the King's apartments, the dining room, and the music room.

The panels date from that time. It is still possible nowadays to, see, opposite the windows, doors opening under the cornice and into the musicians' gallery. The latter was built between the first and ground-floor above the adjoining Buffet Room.

During the 1750 construction work, Louis XV made this room the antechamber of his apartments.

After being the Officers' Room under Napoleon 1, it was used as a Billiards Room by Louis-Philippe.

The present furniture mainly dates from the Emperor's time. The gilded green bronze table with a green Vosges granite top is not of the same period but its neoclassical style makes it quite remarkable.

13 - LOUIS-PHILIPPE'S FAMILY DRAWING ROOM

By visiting this room, one can imagine perfectly what Louis-Philippe's family life was like. He ordered the creation of one single room out of the two which had existed there previously.

The two rooms had been Louis XIV's second Antechamber until 1691, then the Games Room and the Duchesse de Bourgogne's Antechamber, also called the Slumber Room. Under Napoleon I, the former Games Room became the High Officers' Room, and the Slumber-Room

Louis-Philippe's
Family Drawing Room

the Room of the Princes. One knows how much Louis-Philippe liked the familiar gatherings in which the Queen and the Princes and Princesses, his children, took part.

This was the reason why the King thought of creating the Grand Drawing Room which still exists nowadays, with its round tables with numbered drawers in which each Princess kept her needlework (tapestry or crochet), and its comfortable sofas.

The Family Room contains a collection of paintings dating from Louis XIV; the rooms in which they once hung are no longer to be seen in their original state.

The paintings by Bon de Boulogne and Louis de Boulogne once adorned the Games Antechamber while those by René-Antoine Houasse had been delivered for Louis XIV's Billiards Room and François Verdier's for Trianon-in-the-Woods.

The paintings in this room depict mythological themes inspired by Ovids's "Metamorphoses" and portray, in particular, the legends of Minerva and Venus.

On the upper section of the large wall hang paintings by René-Antoine Houasse (from right to left): Minerva watering her horses, Minerva and Perseus, Minerva and Tiresias and Minerva and Arachne.

Over the fireplace, a work by Bon de Boulogne, Mercury and Venus, hangs between four paintings by Verdier (Venus and Adonis, Venus, Cupid and Adonis, The Birth of Adonis and Argus leading Io in the form of a cow).

In a painting above the entrance, Bon de Boulogne has depicted Nature and the Elements. The three other overdoors are by Louis de Boulogne and portray Venus, Hymen and Cupid (right wall), and opposite, Venus and Adonis (window side) and Jupiter turned into a bull.

"Venus, Cupid and Adonis"
by Verdier

161

14 - THE SUNSET DRAWING ROOM

The decoration of this rooms was the work of Lassurance. It dates from 1699, a time when the Duchesse de Bourgogne had her bedroom here. This is one of the few rooms of Trianon in which some of the wooden panels were gilded. This is also one of the first rooms of the residence where arched mirrors were used.

The Sunset Drawing Room had no special use in the 18th century but it became Napoleon 1's State Drawing Room under the Empire. The room has been restored to the Imperial state and is an excellent example of the luxury lavished by the Emperor on his palaces, the Tuileries and St-Cloud as well as Trianon. This luxury is enhanced by the quality of the furniture gathered here: ebony and bronze cabinets made by Jacob-Desmalter for the State Cabinet in the Tuileries in 1809 and brought here in 1811; candelabra and vessels adorned with malachites given to Napoleon 1 by the Czar, Alexander 1; giltwood seats delivered by Jacob-Desmalter. As for the pictures, only two of them come from this room as it was under Louis XIV: "Apollo and Tethys" and "Clytie changed into a Sunflower" by Charles de Lafosse.

"Clytie changed into a Sunflower"
162 *by Charles de Lafosse*

The Sunset Drawing Room

15 - THE COOL DRAWING ROOM

Like the Drawing Room of the Springs and the Garden Drawing Room, this room is the continuation of the Gallery by its decoration. Four works by Martin depict views of the Palace of Versailles; the other paintings (three by Jouvenet, one by Bertin) were also in this room, which was used as a State Cabinet under Louis XIV by the Duchesse de Bourgogne.

Under the Empire, this room was the Council Chamber and it was still used as such under the Resto-

The Cool
Drawing Room

"Versailles seen from Montbauron"
by J.-B. Martin

ration. Charles X's last Ministerial Council on his way into exile took place here. The Council table and the Sovereign's armchair have disappeared but the filing cabinets, chair and the folding stools, the regulator-clock and the barometer-thermometer are still here.

16 - THE GALLERY

In the *Grand Siècle,* every château had to have a gallery which was used for festivities at the same time as a hall and a passage and could even be used as a Games Room. Besides its official character the Trianon Gallery is particulary intesting because it shows us the groves of Versailles and Trianon at the end of Louis XIV's reign in twenty-one paintings by Cotelle, two by Allegrain and one by Martin. Some of them (those by Cotelle) contain mythological figures; the others represent the members of Court walking in the gardens. The bas-relief figures of children on the wainscoting in the simulated transepts are the work of Lespingola.

As for the furniture which, here too, dates from the Empire, it is in perfect harmony with the decoration of the wainscoting: the console table and folding stools are designed with great rigour and majesty. The chande-

liers which were made for this room under Napoleon I are adorned with crystal from the Mont-Cenis Manufactory.

Model ships were placed on the console table under Napoleon and replaced by precious vases under Louis-Philippe. It was also during Louis-Philippe's reign, when the Gallery was used as a Dining Room, that the two Languedoc marble drink coolers made for the Buffet Room in 1750 were brought here. In the 19th century the paintings were replaced by historical canvasses. The room was restored to its former state in 1913.

17 - THE DRAWING ROOM GARDEN

The name of this Drawing Room is very recent, dating from the end of the last century. It was decorated under Louis XIV by the sculptor Lespingola. The painting represent the parterres of Versailles. Portico was played here under Louis XIV but the room became a billiards room under Louis XV and it continued to be used as such under Napoleon I. It was Louis-Philippe who made it a reception room. The paintings are by Crépin and were placed here in the early 19th century.

19 - THE DRAWING ROOM OF THE SPRINGS

The name of the room comes from the Garden of the Springs on to which its windows opened and which has since gone. This is one of the last creations of Louis XIV's reign (1713). It is also the last of the four rooms whose painted decoration was partly devoted to the gardens of Versailles. In the 17th century it was the first room of Madame de Maintenon's apartments. In the next century it was Madame de Pompadour's then Marie-Antoinette's State Cabinet. Napoleon 1 later used it as a Map-Room and Louis-Philippe as a Library.

The Garden
Drawing Room

The 17th century pictorial décor of the Grand Trianon is fortunately still in existence and most of it has been returned here. The is a large number o paintings of mythological subjects, revealing Louis XIV's taste in art. However, the most interesting are the ''views'' of the château and gardens of Versailles by Martin, Cotelle and Allegrain which hang in the Gallery as well as the Cool Drawing- Room and the Drawing-Room of the Springs. The detailed portrayals they offer are precious visual accounts of the past.

Pierre-Denis Martin:
The Grand Canal (fragment)

The Drawing Room
of the Springs

167

"Zephyr and Flora"
by Antoine Coypel

20 - THE EMPEROR'S ANTECHAMBER

This room is the first in the Emperor's private apartments. Unlike the rest of the residence, the walls are not adorned with wooden panels but with silks, the designs of which were commissioned by Napoleon 1. Most of the paint-

The Emperor's Antechamber

ings constituted the mural decoration of these rooms in the 17th century but were set into the walls at that time.

This cabinet, also called the Sunrise Cabinet, was Madame de Maintenon's State Bedchamber until 1701, when it became her State Cabinet. In the 18th century it was Madame de Pompadour's, then Marie-Antoinette's bedchamber.

Napoleon 1 used it as his Cabinet until 1812, when it was given its present size and became the Secretary's Cabinet. Under Louis-Philippe this room, like the ones to follow, belonged to the Princesses' apartments.

21 - THE EMPEROR'S STUDY

This room was Madame de Maintenon's State Bedchamber from 1702 to 1715.

In the 18th century, it was divided into two and did not regain its former size until 1812, when it became the Emperor's Study.

The decoration was then completely changed and we have here a unique example of the complete Empire style in Trianon: the ceiling, the fireplace and the over doors, with their military trophies, date from that time, as do the green and gold fabrics, the two filing cabinets by Jacob-Des-

malter, the clock, the wall-brackets and the andirons. The seats were at Saint-Cloud and the table at the Élysée under the Empire. The following room was Madame de Maintenon's former retiring cabinet, then that of Louis XV and, finally, of Louis XVI.

The room regained its former size under Napoleon I who had it made into his Bathroom, which we see today, its walls and seats covered in white cotton damask and its bath covered with a green carpet.

The Emperor's
Study 169

23 - THE EMPEROR'S BEDCHAMBER

This room was not given its present size until 1750, when it became Louis XV's Council Cabinet. The panels and the fireplace date from that time. Louis XVI had his Private Cabinet here and Napoleon 1 made it his bedroom. It was still used as a bedroom by Louis-Philippe's daughter Louise, Queen of the Belgians, before it became the King's Cabinet. The room has been restored in the Empire style: the seats and the bed were found again and the chest of drawers and the desk delivered by Baudouin returned to their original cetting; finally, the magnificent buff lilac and silver wall hangings were rewoven according to the original designed for Empress Josephine at the Tuileries and used again here by Napoleon in 1809.

24 - THE EMPEROR'S BREAKFAST PARLOUR

Nothing remains of Louis XIV's former Buffet Room which opened into the Music Room at that time.

As in the preceding room, the decoration dates from 1750, when Louis XV made this his bedchamber also used by Louis XVI.

Napoleon 1 made it his Breakfast Parlour, that is to say a small dining room.

The wall-hangings of "cheap damask" and the seats date from Napoleon's time. The needlework table, pedestal table and writing desk, although in the Directory or Empire style, were not brought to Trianon until Louis-Philippe's time. The overdoors are by Restout and Oudry.

25 - THE EMPEROR'S FAMILY DRAWING ROOM

Like the other rooms of the right front section of the building, which we now enter, the Empe-ror's Family Drawing Room oc-cupies the site of Louis XIV's theatre, which was destroyed in 1703 when the Sovereign decided to have his new (and third) apart-ment created here.

The Emperor's
Breakfast Parlour

The Emperor's
Family Drawing Room

This room became the King's Antechamber; it had two windows opening on to the gardens and three opening on to the courtyard. It was then that the cornice with its military and musical trophies was carved.

In 1750, Louis XV had the Antechamber transformed into a Games Room. Oudry's painting of "Plenty" and the magnificent violet brecciated marble fireplace also date from Louis XV's time. The furniture was delivered by Jacob-Desmalter for this room when Napoleon 1 made it his Family Drawing-Room also used as a Games-Room.

Louis-Philippe used it for the same purpose until 1845, when it became the reception-room for the Queen of the Belgians.

26 - THE QUEEN OF THE BELGIANS' BEDCHAMBER

When Louis XVI had the theatre destroyed, he chose the site of the present room as his bedchamber and private Cabinet.

It was Louis XV who connected the two into a dining-room, in 1750.

Louis-Philippe had it transformed into a bedroom for the King and Queen of the Belgians in 1845. The present furniture was brought here at that time.

The Queen of the Belgian's Bedchamber

This room is followed by two more which occupy the site of Louis XIV's Council Chamber. Under Louis XV, this became a buffet room for which the two drink-coolers, now in the Gallery, were executed.

The last two rooms to be visited in the Grand Trianon are two ante-chambers which have been newly decorated and adorned with four paintings by Noël Coypel. In the first antechamber, the visitor may admire "Deianira Sending Nessus' Tunic to Hercules" and in the other, "Plenty", "The Fight between Hercules and Achelous", "The Wounded Nessus Giving his Tunic to Deianira".

THE GRAND TRIANON GARDENS

For Louis XIV, the gardens at Trianon, like those of all his residences, had an extremely important rôle to play. Those of Versailles are inspired by a whole mythological symbolism which is visible everywhere. At Trianon, however, there is little ornamentation based on Antiquity; the gardens are a simple but remarkable homage to nature itself.

Although they were badly treated towards the end of the 18th century, the original layout of the Grand Trianon gardens still exists as it was designed by Le Bouteux, the nephew of Le Nôtre, at the time of the Porcelain Trianon. When Trianon was rebuilt, all the gardens were rearranged by Le Nôtre who worked on them until his death in 1700.

Then Hardouin-Mansart completed certain of the groves. It was not until 1704 that some of the sculpture and lead from the groves destroyed at Versailles began to be placed here.

Seven steps lead from the Peristyle to the Upper Garden, flanked, to the right, by the Gallery, and, to the left, by a terrace overlooking the northern extremity of the small arm of the Grand Canal.

The Upper Garden and the Right Wing 173

The Upper Garden is adorned with two red Languedoc marble pools in the centre of which are groups
of children by Girardon formerly in the Banquet
Hall destroyed in 1706. These fountains are in the
centre of parterres whose Louis XIV floral embroidery was simplified under Louis XVI. The Lower
Garden contains a pool decorated with a group by
Marsy, "The Child surrounded by Grapes", situated in the middle of four parterres. It was here that,
under Louis XIV, the orange-trees and flowery
shrubs, so greatly admired at the time, were set out.

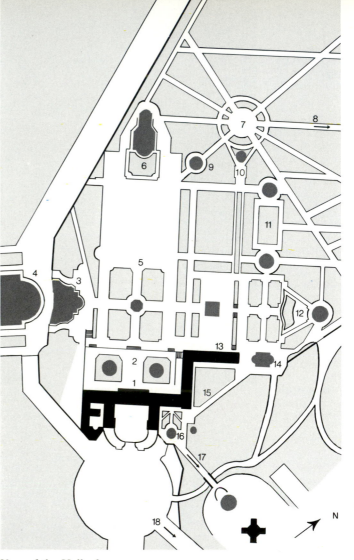

Vase of the Hall of
Classical Statues

PLAN OF THE GARDENS OF THE GRAND TRIANON

1. The Peristyle
2. The Upper Parterre
3. Horse-Shoe Fountain and Slope
4. Small Arm of the Grand Canal
5. The Lower Garden
6. The Mirror Fountain
7. The Small Star
8. To the Great Star and the Queen's Star
9. The Round Fountain
10. The Water Buffet
11. The Green Hall
12. The Hall of Classical Statues
13. The Trianon in the Woods
14. Pool with two half-moons
15. Garden of the Springs
16. The King's Garden
17. To the Small Trianon
18. Marie-Antoinette's Hamlet

To the north spreads a little wood with three principal "Stars": the Small Star, the Great Star and the Queen's Star. From the Mirror Fountain, an avenue leads northwards to the grove of the Round Pool, situated in the axis of the Garden Drawing-Room. Beyond the Round Pool, in the axis of the Pavilion of Trianon-in-the-Woods stands the famous Water Buffet designed by Hardouin-Mansart in 1703 to replace the cascade of the Porcelain Trianon. It was built in white Carrara and red Languedoc marble, and adorned with sculptures by

At the south end of the Lower Garden, a balustrade overlooks the Horseshoe Fountain (built by Le Vau from 1678 to 1679). It is part of a large stairway leading in two symmetrical parts to the north arm of the Grand Canal.

The Peristyle seen from the gardens

In the axis of the Peristyle a wide avenue leads to the Mirror Fountain (with bowls on two levels) adorned with groups of children. On its rims, two dragons by Hardy frame the edge of the upper level. Beyond this fountain stands the "Knifegrinder", a marble statue in the classical style, set against trees which round off this view of the gardens.

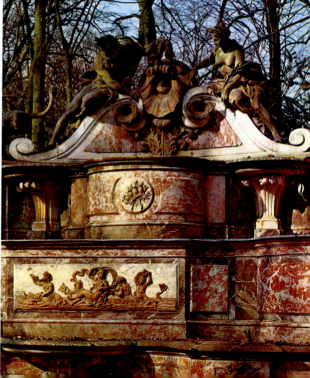

The Water Buffet

Van Clève, Mazière, Le Lorrain, Poirier and Hardy, with Neptune and Amphitrite as its central theme.

From the Water Buffet, we go back to Trianon-in-the-Woods through the Green Hall and, symmetrical to the Horseshoe in relation to the axis of the Gallery, we find the Hall of Classical Statues or Amphitheatre. Although it has been altered, it has kept its pool adorned with four nymphs and, at regular intervals along the semicircle, twenty-five busts copied from classical models.

After going through the end of Trianon-in-the-Woods, where we find a pool with two half-moons adorned with a faun attributed to Marsy we come to the second part of the gardens of Trianon. Situated in the angle formed by the Gallery and the Trianon-in-the-Woods wing, the Garden of Springs was a sort of Louis XIVth prefiguration of the ''English Garden''. The springs were unfortunately removed in 1776 and replaced by a simple parterre. Only the group of ''Cupid on a dolphin'' by Marsy, placed here in 1704, still remains. Beyond this, and formerly separated from the rest of the gardens by a little wall, lies the former ''King's Garden''. It was also very roughly treated in the 18th century and yet it has kept its original appea-

rance more successfully in particular in the middle of the ''embroidered'' parterres with the fountain adorned with two Cupids, by Tubi. In the *Grand Siècle,* this garden, which was strictly reserved for the King, was adorned with the rarest and most fragrant flowers. To the east of the King's Garden, a pathway leads over a bridge to the Small Trianon.

The French
Pavilion

THE SMALL TRIANON

The sovereigns of Versailles always cared lovingly for the Trianon estates, the privileged site of their pleasure and leisure, the realm of Flora herself.

Louis XV showed no great interest in the Grand Trianon, preferring the adjoining land which lay beyond the King's Garden, where botanical gardens were laid out at his request. In order to be on the spot to follow the experiments that took place there, the King decided to have new buildings created. The "New Menagerie", was completed by Gabriel in 1749 to shelter indigenous animals for selection of the species. It was provided with a farm, a dovecot, a henhouse, a cowshed and a dairy.

Another parterre garden was then created to the east. In 1750, the French Pavilion was erected in the middle of this parterre. Louis XV would retire to take a rest there on his way back from his many visits to the New Menagerie. It has a cross-shaped ground-plan with four cabinets surrounding a large circular drawing-room. There is a charming simplicity about the exterior: the monotony of the façades is relieved by the shape of the cabinets jutting out and a balustrade adorned with sculptures, groups of children and vases. The circular drawing-room is provided with a sumptuous floor of marble slabs, while the walls lined with wainscoting by Verberckt are rythmed with eight Corinthian columns. The cornice is decorated with a frieze of farmyard animals recalling the nearby Menagerie.

As early as 1761, Madame de Pompadour had suggested to Louis XV that a small château be erected in the French Garden.

During one of his stays at the Small Trianon, in May 1774, Louis XV felt for the first time the symptoms of the disease from which he was going to die. As soon as he became King, Louis XVI presented the estate to the Queen, who soon made Trianon her favourite residence.

The project was be carried out by Gabriel and the Small Trianon is Gabriel's most successful work of art. The building erected on a square ground plan comprises a basement, a main floor, and an attic storey surmounted with a balustrade.

The French Garden and the Small Trianon

Owing to variations in the ground level, the basement is only visible on the Main Courtyard side and on the side facing The Temple of Love. The east and north façades are simply decorated with a succession of large windows. The main façade, on the French Pavilion side, is adorned with a series of lofty Corinthian columns and that looking on to the Belvedere with pilasters.

THE STAIRCASE

Light pours in on to the staircase leading to the main floor. The two stone flights of stairs have a magnificent wrought-iron banister bearing Marie-Antoinette's gilded monogram. The beautiful Louis XVI lantern was hung in 1811 at the request of the Empress Marie-Louise. The landing gives access to the antechamber on the right-hand side, whereas another staircase, which is smaller, leads on to the attic apartments, on the left-hand side.

THE ANTECHAMBER

Situated in the south-west corner of the château, this room which has a French window opening out, fittingly enough, on to the French Garden, forms an entrance to the apartment on the main floor. On either side of the door leading to the Dining-Room, Gabriel had placed two earthenware heaters; in the course of the 19th century, they were replaced by wood panelling carved by Verbeckt for the Cool Drawing Room (a pavilion in the French Garden, no longer in existence).

LOUIS XV's DINING ROOM

Restoration work has returned its former splendour and luxury to this room. The sculpture and carving of the fireplace and the panelling are by

The Staircase
of the Small Trianon

Guibert; here again, the motifs stand out in white against a pale green background. The frames of the mirror and the pictures have been reconstructed after designs found on the walls. All the paintings were commissioned by Louis XV and executed between 1769 and 1777.

The four paintings above the doors evoke the divinities of flowers and fruit; they are the work of Belle and Monnet. On either side of the doors are four original pictures specially ordered to hang there. They represent: "Agriculture" by Lagrenée, "Hunting" by Vien, "Fishing" by Doyen and "The Wine Harvest" by Hallé. Furniture of quality has been selected to recall the former comfort and elegance of the room.

The two large candelabra of chased gilt bronze were originally delivered to Saint-Cloud for Louis XVI's Games Room. Two chests of drawers in mahogany and gilded bronze, attributed to Carlin, have been placed between the windows. The twenty-two chairs were delivered by Séné in 1790, for the King's Games-Room at Compiègne. They are of carved gilded wood and have been upholstered with crimson damask to match the Tours silk curtains especially woven for this room.

Louis XV's
Dining Room

THE BILLIARDS ROOM

Louis XV's Small Dining Room, which became Marie-Antoinette's Billiards Room, again has its 18th century colour scheme. Among the furniture, we should notice the chest of drawers by Riesener, which bears the marks of Marie-Antoinette's furniture repository, and the two Louis XVI vases made of ostrich eggs. The seats are the work of Dupain. Like the windows, they are covered in crimson Tours silk.

THE BEDCHAMBER

Marie-Antoinette decided to make Louis XV's former Cabinet her bedchamber. The carving on the wainscoting is a reminder of the King's taste for botany and an experimental garden on to which the windows used to open.

When the wainscoting has been restored to its 18th century state, the "pastoral motif" furniture, delivered by Jacob in 1787, will again be placed in this chamber for which it was created. This suite consists of two armchairs, two chairs, a stool and a firescreen.

The wainscoting, carved by Rode, was painted in natural tones by Chaillot de Prusse in imitation of cane; it is adorned with flowers and pastoral symbols.

Fortunately, the original bedspread of white cashmere embroidered with flowers of coloured wool has been preserved until today. The "pulpit" bedstead which belonged to the suite of furniture disappeared during the 19th century. However, the two tables delivered by Schwerdfeger and made especially for this room have been returned here, together with the clock.

THE BOUDOIR

From the Bedchamber, one may catch a glimpse of the Queen's Boudoir, which is not open to visitors. It was created in 1787 on the site of a former staircase and was the only room to be specially decorated for Marie-Antoinette. The wood-panelling is carved with delicate arbesques, probably executed after designs by Mique, surrounding the Queen's monogram. By means of an ingenious device which has been recently restored, the windows can be covered by large mirrors drawn up from the floor.

THE MUSIC ROOM

This room was mostly frequented by Marie-Antoinette's entourage of relatives or close friends. Madame Campan, the Queen's faithful attendant, relates in her Memoirs that Marie-Antoinette "decided on the way of life in this château: when she entered the room, the ladies did not have to leave the pianoforte or their tapestry; nor did the gentlemen relinquish their games, of billiards or trick-track". Here, as in the dining-room, Guibert gave of all his talent as a sculptor. One should admire the wood-panelling, restored in 1975, and the fireplace. The triple-coloured damask (the same as in the Queen's time) and the furniture, almost all placed here by Empress Eugénie, evoke the art of living in simplicity and calm, now lost, which was that of Trianon.

The Music Room

MARIE-ANTOINETTE'S THEATRE

Marie-Antoinette's Theatre, erected next to the Small Trianon, was completed by Mique in 1780. Skilfully concealed amidst the foliage of the trees, the Theatre may be recognized by its entrance porch decorated with Ionic columns and surmounted with a pediment sculpted by Deschamps. The interior décor recalls that of the Opera in the Palace of Versailles. The room is u-shaped; above the stage, there is a cartouche bearing Marie-Antoinette's monogram. The colour sheme is mainly blue and gold, with banisters painted violet in the balcony.

The original ceiling, painted by Lagrenée, depicted "Apollo in the Company of the Muses and Graces".

Acting was one of the Queen's hobbies. Of course, her little troupe was composed only of close friends or relatives. As for the audience, admittance was restricted to members of the Royal Family and a few servants before whom several plays and comic-operas were performed. The little theatre among the trees was left undisturbed for centuries to come, as a silent token of the bygone charm and grace of the last Queen of France.

Marie-Antoinette's Theatre

THE SMALL TRIANON
THE INTERIOR

Except for the French Garden, the parterres of the Small Trianon are very different now. Instead of the winding alleys, the grassy meadows and the clusters of trees, there used to be a well-kept plot of ground in which the gardener Claude Richard devoted himself for more than thirty years to the culture of the rarest varieties of plants and trees: pineapples, aloes, coffee, geraniums and the strawberry, not very well known at the time. From 1775 onwards, Claude Richard's plantations were dug up. The new gardens, modelled on those then to be seen in the Count of Caraman's estate, were designed in the Anglo-Chinese style, then very much in fashion. They were laid out by Mique, on the advice of Hubert-Robert and Claude Richard. A small rivulet issuing forth from a pond was to wind its way through hilly ground adorned with patches of grass, rocks, and rare species of trees, with a few light constructions here and there.

In 1777, a neo-classical pavilion was erected by Mique on the uppermost hillock, commanding a view over the pond. The "Belvedere", octagonal in shape and surrounded by four steps flanked with sphinxes. The sculptures on the pediments depict rustic pleasures, while the bas-reliefs symbolize the four seasons. The interior is paved with a marble mosaic. The arabesques on the stucco walls were painted by Le Riche, while the clear sky with fleeting clouds on the cupola is the work of Lagrenée.

The Temple of Love was erected by Mique on an islet of the river, opposite the windows of the Queen's Chamber. This "Temple" consists of twelve Corinthian columns of white marble, standing on a circular pedestal of seven steps, and surmounted by a cupola. In the middle stands a copy, executed by Bouchardon, of "Cupid carving his bow out of Hercules' club"; the original, carved in 1746, is now in the Louvre.

*The Rock Pavilion
or Belvedere*

THE HAMLET
(1783-1785)

During the second half of the 18th century, Jean-Jacques Rousseau's theories about recapturing the natural simplicity of life were very much in favour. These new ideas prompted Marie-Antoinette to create the "Hamlet" in order to imitate the simplicity of peasant life as she saw it.

The Hamlet is a kind of fairyland village on the banks of the Great Trianon lake. It was built by Mique between 1783 and 1785 and comprised twelve houses.

We suggest that the visitor to the Gardens of the Small Trianon begin with the Belvedere, cross over the bridge, then turn right and follow the winding banks of the river.

A leisurely stroll will eventually lead him to the Great Lake, whose motionless surface is adorned with clusters of reeds and a wealth of white water lilies; the cobwalled, thatched cottages line the other bank.

Resuming his walk on the left of the lake, the visitor will first discover the "Processing Dairy" and the Marlborough Tower with the fishery underneath. The "Preparation Dairy" and the Barn, which was used as a Ballroom, once stood nearby.

"Marie-Antoinette with a Rose"
by Elisabeth Vigée-Lebrun

As one follows the sandy pathway one passes close by the Caretaker's House and the Dovecot. Then, after crossing the little bridge, one arrives at the Queen's Cottage, the main construction in the village. This cottage consists of two buildings linked by a gallery which is reached by an external spiral staircase. The steps of the staircase and the wooden gallery are decorated with flower pots of blue and white earthenware bearing the Queen's cipher.

The constructions chosen to decorate the landscapes imagined by Richard Mique were first created in the form of small-scale models. These "minutely detailed three dimensional models which followed a tradition which went back to Louis XIV" were intended "to give an idea of the desired effect before building began". The models of the Temple of Love and the Belvedere "presented to Marie-Antoinette must have been charming objects which, one regrets, were not preserved".

Pierre de Nolhac

The Temple of Love

"The pleasure of strolling through all the farmyard buildings of the Hamlet, of seeing the cows being milked, of fishing in the lake, enchanted the Queen" (wrote Madame Campan). It was, in fact, a real little farm: "the gardens were cultivated, the fields ploughed, the trees were pruned and the fruit gathered. From the gallery of her cottage, (the Queen could see) the donkey taking the corn to be ground at the mill... the washerwomen beating the linen on the banks of the pond" Pierre de Nolhac.

The meticulously decorated interiors of the cottages in the Hamlet contrast with the natural simplicity of the exteriors. The Queen's Cottage, comprising drawing rooms and a library, were of great luxury. The Mill itself, a delightful construction right out of a fairytale, also had an elegant room.

The Dovecot and the caretaker's House

The Mill
on a summer evening

PLAN OF TRIANON

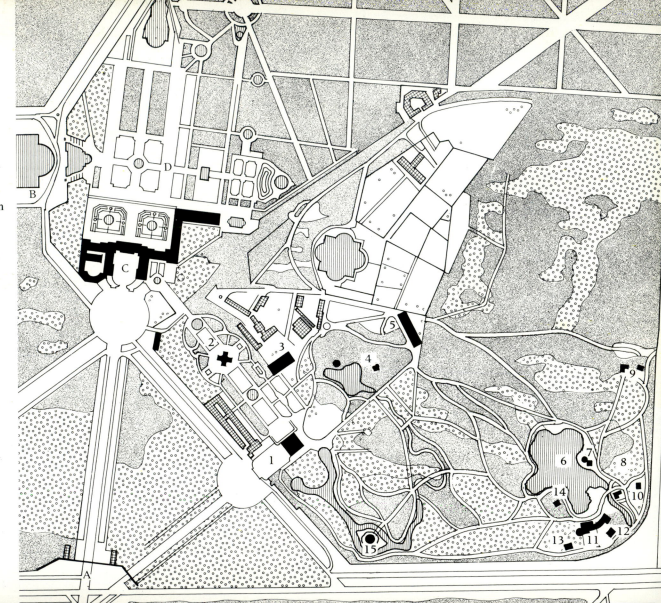

Created for the Sun King's leizure, the lands of Trianon were, at first, a garden of delight, entirely dedicated to the cult of Flora. Then, during the century of the encyclopedia it became a botanical garden in which Louis XV took a keen interest. This scientific creation was sacrificed to make way for the romantic garden we see today, designed to suit Marie-Antoinette's taste. It was at Trianon, where she would rest in the grotto during a solitary walk, that the Queen was surprised by the news of the arrival at the château of the revolutionary mob of Parisians. "She returned hastily on foot through the gardens", leaving Trianon forever on 5th October 1789. The following day, the royal family and the Court left Versailles permanently.

Today's visitor should not be too nostalgic for the heady perfumes of Louis XIV's flowers; those of today, too, have their charm and, while the fountains no longer play except at certain times, one should listen to their murmur evoke the sound of past festivities.

And when, at the end of his day at Versailles, he passes beneath the tall, century-old trees of Trianon, let him remember that the one who planted them did not have the joy of seeing them flourish.

CHRONOLOGY

1075 First mention of the name of Versailles in Philippe I's Records.

1275 Gilles, Baron of Versailles, relinquishes his rights to Trianon to the Abbot of Saint-Germain.

1575 Albert de Gondi, Baron of Marly and Marshall of Retz, buys the Manor of Versailles.

1624 Louis XIII orders a hunting pavilion to be built on the small hill of Versailles.

1631 Louis XIII commissions Philibert Le Roy to build a small palace on the site of the hunting pavilion. Work is completed in 1634.

1660 On the 7th June, the marriage of Louis XIV and Marie-Thérèse, Infanta of Spain. They go to Versailles on 25th October.

1661 Death of the Prime Minister, Cardinal Mazarin, and beginning of Louis XIV's personal rule. Colbert is named Director of Finances. Birth of the Grand Dauphin.

1663 The architect Le Vau builds the first Orangery and begins the Menagerie.

1664 In May, the King holds the festivities called *Pleasures of the Enchanted Island*.

1665 The first statues appear in the gardens.
The façades of the Marble Courtyard are adorned with busts. The Grotto of Tethys is begun.

1668 Adoption of Le Vau's project to enlarge the palace on the garden side by a "stone envelope".
On 18th July, Louis XIV holds the "Great Royal Entertainment" for his amazed courtiers.

1667 Digging begins on the Grand Canal.

1670 Creation of the "Porcelain Trianon". The first eight groups of statues are placed along the Water Avenue.

1672 The Bathing Apartment on the ground floor of the new palace is begun. Work begins on the Ambassadors' Staircase.

1674 Year of the "great commission" of 24 statues for the gardens.
The last of the three great celebrations held by Louis XIV at Versailles.

1678 Jules Hardouin-Mansart designs plans for enlarging the palace. The garden terrace is removed to make room for the Hall of Mirrors.

1681 Completion of decoration of the State Apartments.

1682 On 16th May, Louis XIV decrees that Versailles is henceforth to be the official court residence and the seat of government.

1684 Completion of the Hall of Mirrors. Construction of the Orangery.
On 10th April, Anne-Marie d'Orléans, Louis XIV's niece, marries Victor-Amadeus II, Duc de Savoie. Work begins to divert the waters of the Eure to Versailles.

1685 Construction of the North Wing begins.

1686 The Marly Machine begins to bring the waters of the Seine to Versailles. Creation of the Maison Royale at Saint-Cyr, an institution for poor young ladies of the nobility.

1687 Construction of the "Marble Trianon".

1689 In December, Louis XIV orders all the silverware and silver furniture of Versailles to be melted down.

1699 Construction of the newest and last chapel, by Mansart, begins. Girardon's "Rape of Persephone" is placed in the Colonnade Grove.

1706 Morand's automaton clock is delivered and placed in the Mercury Drawing Room.

1710 Completion of the Royal Chapel.
On 15th February, birth of the Duc d'Anjou, (the future Louis XV), third son of the Duc de Bourgogne.

1715 On 1st September, death of Louis XIV at 8.15 in the morning.
On 9th September, Louis XV leaves Versailles for Vincennes.

1722 On 15th June, Louis XV returns to make Versailles his residence.

1725 On 5th April, after breaking off her engagement to Louis XV, the Infanta, Dona Maria-Anna-Victoria, leaves Versailles for Spain.

1738 Large-scale work to rearrange the Private Cabinets begins.

1747 Marriage of the Dauphin to Maria-Josepha of Saxony.

1754 On 23rd August, birth of Louis-Auguste of France, the Duc de Berry (Louis XVI).

1755 Transformation of the King's Cabinet, or the Ministers' Council Chamber.

1770 On 16th May, marriage of the Dauphin to Marie-Antoinette of Lorraine, Archduchess of Austria.
Opening of the Royal Opera built by Gabriel.

1771 Project for reconstructing all palace façades facing the town. The Louis XV Wing is begun by Gabriel.

1774 On 10th May, Louis XV dies of smallpox at Versailles.

1783 Signature of the Treaties which put an end to the war and confirm the independence of the United States of America. Construction begins on Marie-Antoinette's Hamlet at Trianon.

1789 On 5th May, opening of the Estates General in the *Salle des Menus Plaisirs*.
On 6th October, after the invasion of the palace, the Royal Family and the whole Court leave Versailles for Paris, never to return.

1792 On 20th October, following a proposition by the *député* Roland, the Convention orders the sale of a large part of the royal furniture.

1793 On 21st January, Louis XVI, condemned to death, is decapitated in Paris.
On 16th October, Marie-Antoinette is led to the scaffold.

1806 Napoleon I orders plans to be designed for restoring and enlarging the château, which he intends to make his residence.

1814 Louis XVIII orders all the palace apartments to be "restored to a habitable state".

1833 On 1st September, King Louis-Philippe orders the transformation of the palace of Versailles into a Museum of French History.

1837 On 10th June, inauguration of the Museum of Versailles.

1871 On 18th January, the German Empire is proclaimed in the Hall of Mirrors.
On 12th March, the National Assembly meets in the Opera which has been transformed for the occasion.

1919 On 28th June 1919, the Allied Powers and Germany sign the Treaty of Versailles ending the first world war.

1957 Reopening of the entirely restored Royal Opera.

1975 Restoration of the Queen's Bedchamber.

1978 Reopening of the Consulate and Empire Rooms.

1980 Restoration of the furniture in the King's Bedchamber and the Hall of Mirrors.

1982 June 4, 5, 6 : Summit of the Industrialized Countries. Marble Courtyard is relev elled.

1984 Staircase designed by Gabriel is built.

1986 On the ground floor of the Central building, restoration of the Lower Gallery and the 18th century apartments.

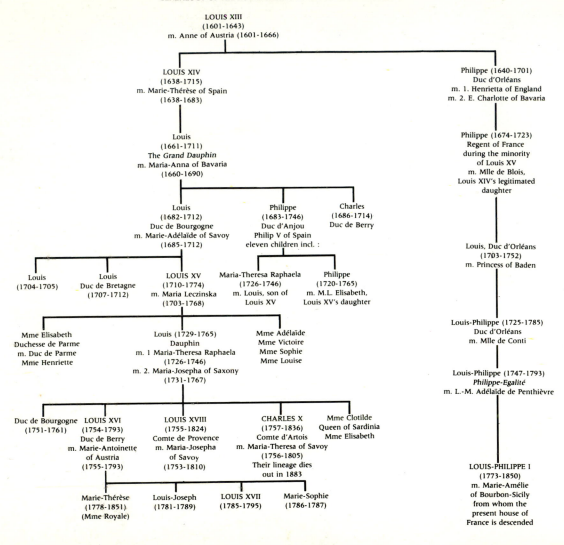

LOUIS XIII
(1601-1643)
m. Anne of Austria (1601-1666)

LOUIS XIV
(1638-1715)
m. Marie-Thérèse of Spain
(1638-1683)

Philippe (1640-1701)
Duc d'Orléans
m. 1. Henrietta of England
m. 2. E. Charlotte of Bavaria

Louis
(1661-1711)
The *Grand Dauphin*
m. Maria-Anna of Bavaria
(1660-1690)

Philippe (1674-1723)
Regent of France
during the minority
of Louis XV
m. Mlle de Blois,
Louis XIV's legitimated
daughter

Louis
(1682-1712)
Duc de Bourgogne
m. Marie-Adélaïde of Savoy
(1685-1712)

Philippe
(1683-1746)
Duc d'Anjou
Philip V of Spain
eleven children incl. :

Charles
(1686-1714)
Duc de Berry

Louis, Duc d'Orléans
(1703-1752)
m. Princess of Baden

Louis
(1704-1705)

Louis
Duc de Bretagne
(1707-1712)

LOUIS XV
(1710-1774)
m. Maria Leczinska
(1703-1768)

Maria-Theresa Raphaela
(1726-1746)
m. Louis, son of
Louis XV

Philippe
(1720-1765)
m. M.L. Elisabeth,
Louis XV's daughter

Louis-Philippe (1725-1785)
Duc d'Orléans
m. Mlle de Conti

Mme Elisabeth
Duchesse de Parme
m. Duc de Parme
Mme Henriette

Louis (1729-1765)
Dauphin
m. 1 Maria-Theresa Raphaela
(1726-1746)
m. 2. Maria-Josepha of Saxony
(1731-1767)

Mme Adélaïde
Mme Victoire
Mme Sophie
Mme Louise

Louis-Philippe (1747-1793)
Philippe-Egalité
m. L.-M. Adélaïde de Penthièvre

Duc de Bourgogne
(1751-1761)

LOUIS XVI
(1754-1793)
Duc de Berry
m. Marie-Antoinette
of Austria
(1755-1793)

LOUIS XVIII
(1755-1824)
Comte de Provence
m. Maria-Josepha
of Savoy
(1753-1810)

CHARLES X
(1757-1836)
Comte d'Artois
m. Maria-Theresa of Savoy
(1756-1805)
Their lineage dies
out in 1883

Mme Clotilde
Queen of Sardinia
Mme Elisabeth

LOUIS-PHILIPPE I
(1773-1850)
m. Marie-Amélie
of Bourbon-Sicily
from whom the
present house of
France is descended

Marie-Thérèse
(1778-1851)
(Mme Royale)

Louis-Joseph
(1781-1789)

LOUIS XVII
(1785-1795)

Marie-Sophie
(1786-1787)